The F/A-18 Hornet Story

The F/A-18 Hornet Story

TONY HOLMES

The
History
Press

Published in the United Kingdom in 2011 by
The History Press
The Mill · Brimscombe Port · Stroud · Gloucestershire · GL5 2QG

British Library Cataloguing in Publication Data
A catalogue record for this book is available from the British Library.

ISBN 978-0-7524-6269 1

Typesetting and origination by The History Press
Printed in China

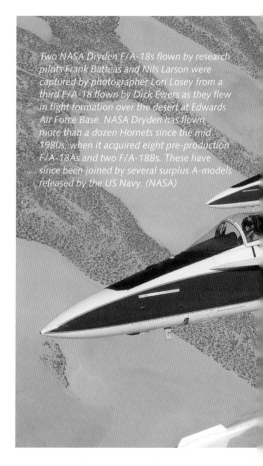

Two NASA Dryden F/A-18s flown by research pilots Frank Batteas and Nils Larson were captured by photographer Lori Losey from a third F/A-18 flown by Dick Ewers as they flew in tight formation over the desert at Edwards Air Force Base. NASA Dryden has flown more than a dozen Hornets since the mid 1980s, when it acquired eight pre-production F/A-18As and two F/A-18Bs. These have since been joined by several surplus A-models released by the US Navy. (NASA)

CONTENTS

ACKNOWLEDGEMENTS

I have been writing about US naval aviation since the mid-1980s, and since that time one aircraft has remained a constant fixture on the flightdecks of America's supercarriers – the F/A-18 Hornet. I saw my first examples when USS *Constellation* (CV-64) visited Fremantle, Western Australia, in July 1985 with Carrier Air Wing Fourteen (CVW-14) embarked. That same month I was fortunate enough to be at Royal Australian Air Force (RAAF) Base Pearce when two 'Aussie' F/A-18Bs visited Western Australia for the first time. Since then, I have photographed the aircraft both on carrier decks and in the air literally across the globe, Hornets have steadily

◀ *Known as 'America's Flagship', USS* Constellation *(CV-64) visited Fremantle, Western Australia, in July 1985 during CVW-14's first deployment with the F/A-18A. This was the first time that the author had seen the Hornet in the flesh. No fewer than 17 of the 20 F/A-18As embarked in CV-64 by VFA-25 and VFA-113 can be seen on the flightdeck in this aerial photograph, taken shortly after the vessel had left its San Diego homeport on 20 February 1985. (US Navy)*

become the dominant aircraft type in US Navy service as other venerable warplanes such as the Tomcat, Viking, Corsair II and Prowler have been retired. Although now in the latter stages of its career, the 'legacy' Hornet – as the original jet has been labelled since the advent of the bigger Super Hornet more than a decade ago – remains a key asset in the arsenal of today's US Navy.

As always when producing a volume such as this one, I call upon my regular contacts for photographs to help illustrate the colourful career of a naval aviation icon. Typically, I have been supplied with a huge number of images, and once again it has been a difficult job to whittle the photographs down to the 115 seen in this book. I would therefore like to thank Bob Archer, Mark Attrill, Steve Davies, Nic Eccles and Andrew McLaughlin at *Australian Aviation* magazine, Jan Jacobs and Doug Siegfried of the Tailhook Association, Philip Jarrett, Jyrki Laukkanen, Chris Lofting, Peter Mersky, Lon Nordeen, Glenn Sands, Pete Scheu, Joerg Stange and Peter Steinemann for their efforts on my behalf.

Tony Holmes
Sevenoaks, Kent

INTRODUCTION

Following the cancellation of the Navy's VFAX lightweight multi-role fighter programme by the US Congress in 1974, the latter recommended that the service should focus on a navalised General Dynamics YF-16 or Northrop YF-17, which had been built for the USAF-sponsored Lightweight Fighter project. Neither of these companies had any experience constructing naval aircraft, so McDonnell Douglas paired up with Northrop and Ling-Temco-Vought (LTV) went into partnership with General Dynamics.

Being twin-engined, the Northrop design had a clear advantage over the YF-16, as the US Navy has always favoured twin-engined combat aircraft when given the choice. Selected to develop their YF-17 prototype into a frontline aircraft on 2 May 1975, Northrop and McDonnell Douglas were initially instructed to build separate F-18 fighter and A-18 attack jets. However, these designs were combined into a single airframe in an effort to cut costs, resulting in production of the F/A-18A Hornet.

The first of 11 full-scale development jets made its maiden flight on 18 November 1978, this machine differing significantly from the lightweight YF-17. Bigger and heavier than the latter, the Hornet was powered by two General Electric F404 turbofans and featured a Hughes AN/APG-65 radar. The airframe had also been

navalised, which meant that a strengthened undercarriage and arrestor hook had been fitted and a folding mechanism installed in the wings.

Production aircraft began reaching the US Navy in May 1980, with the Marine Corps receiving Hornets two years later. A total of 371 A-models and 40 two-seat F/A-18Bs were delivered to the US Navy/Marine Corps up to 1986, when production switched to the F/A-18C/D. The latter featured improved avionics, a new central computer and greater weapons compatibility, and 464 had been built for the US Navy/Marine Corps by the time production ended in 1999. Some 161 of these were two-seat D-models, including 96 Night Attack jets used in the Forward Air Controller (Airborne) mission by the Marine Corps. In 2002-03 200 F/A-18As were

Did you know?

The F/A-18 was developed as the YF-17 by Northrop, who nicknamed it the Cobra. The fighter was given this sobriquet due to the 'hooded' appearance given to the aircraft by its distinctive wing leading-edge root extensions. The jet was officially names the Hornet on 1 March 1977.

upgraded to A+ specification with C-model avionics and returned to frontline service. Making its combat debut over Libya in 1986, the Hornet has seen considerable action from carrier decks and ashore with the Marine Corps.

◀ With its throttles set at MAX and afterburners cut in, an F/A-18C from VFA-136 accelerates to 125 knots in less than two seconds after commencing its catapult launch from the deck of USS Enterprise (CVN-65) in the Northern Arabian Sea in November 2007. (Pete Schue)

The F/A-18 programme can trace its lineage back to the Northrop P-530 Cobra fighter of May 1966, this aircraft being developed by the company's design bureau as the ultimate lightweight fighter. Having devised the highly successful F-5 Freedom Fighter and Tiger II family of fighters, Northrop had plenty of experience when it came to creating such an aircraft.

By 1967 the design that would ultimately become the Hornet was clearly beginning to take shape. The company-funded P-530 study had all the features of a Northrop design – light weight, twin engines, ease of maintenance and the ability to out-fly anything then in service. The fighter featured what was effectively a stretched F-5E fuselage married to small wing leading-edge root extensions, known as LEXs. The wing planform was also virtually identical to that of the F-5, although it was shoulder-mounted and of greater area.

Things then stagnated for the next few years as both the US Air Force and US Navy stated that they had no need for such a design due to the imminent service introduction of the hugely expensive McDonnell Douglas F-15 Eagle and

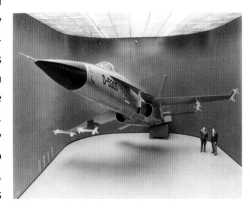

The Northrop P-530 Cobra was the precursor to the F/A-18 Hornet, the aircraft being seen here in mock-up form. This particular model, the P-530-5, was displayed at the 1973 Paris Air Show. (via Philip Jarrett)

Grumman F-14 Tomcat. Both aircraft were large, very capable air superiority fighters, but these attributes had come at a high financial cost that in turn meant reduced production runs. With fewer Eagles and Tomcats being built, there was now a potential requirement for a more cost-effective aircraft to serve alongside these fighters in the frontline. Supporters of this concept argued in the late 1960s for an F-XX fighter programme for the USAF and a VF-XX version for the US Navy. Neither service was keen on this idea, however, as they felt that their 'blue riband' F-14 and F-15 projects were under threat from the cheaper fighter.

However, by 1971 it was clear that both aircraft were financially secure, at which point the USAF and US Navy quickly showed greater interest in the Light Weight Fighter (LWF) technology demonstration programme. The USAF was the first to formally commit to the new aircraft, issuing a request for proposals (RFP) on 6 January 1972 and allocating $12 million from that year's budget to fund the programme. Contenders for the RFP were give a free hand when it came to designing their LWFs, although it was specified that any proposed aircraft should possess a minimum design load factor of 6.5 g and a modest avionics fit. The aircraft was to have a gross weight of less than 20,000lbs and a high thrust-to-weight ratio. Heavy emphasis was placed on the aircraft's speed and agility, rather than its ability to carry a large payload of weapons. Low cost was also desirable, although conversely any new fighter would be expected to incorporate advanced technology!

Did you know?
During flight testing on 11 June 1974, the YF-17 became the first turbojet-powered US type to exceed Mach 1.0 in level flight without the aid of afterburner.

Boeing, General Dynamics, Ling-Temco-Vought and Northrop all submitted designs, with the latter's P-600 candidate being based on a revised version of its P-530 concept. Eventually, this and the General Dynamics submission were chosen for development, and contracts covering the construction of two prototypes of each design were awarded on 13 April 1972. Two weeks later the aim of the LWF programme dramatically changed when Secretary of Defense James Schlesinger announced that he felt it 'appropriate to consider full-scale development and eventual production of an Air Combat Fighter' that would provide an alternative to 'high cost tactical aircraft while maintaining a credible tactical air force'. The Northrop and General Dynamics aircraft had now gone from being 'technology demonstrators' for air force test pilots to 'fool around in' to competing prototypes for the new, and highly lucrative, USAF Air Combat Fighter (ACF) contract. By 1972 the USAF had realised that the F-15 was just too expensive to purchase in the numbers it had originally desired, so it had therefore

decided (or been told by the Secretary of Defense) to adopt a compromise 'hi-lo' mix that saw more costly fighters serving alongside less sophisticated and therefore less expensive machines. The LWF project appeared to offer the perfect solution to the ACF requirement, rather than having to start from scratch with an all-new RFP.

While General Dynamics pressed on with construction of its YF-16 prototype in Fort Worth, Texas, Northrop's LWF, which had been designated the YF-17, was coming together at the company's plant in Hawthorne, California. Rolled out on 9 April 1974, the first YF-17 was subsequently taken by road to Edwards Air Force Base (AFB) and flown for the first time on 9 June. The second prototype made its maiden flight on 21 August, and both jets undertook an accelerated test programme prior to being pitted against the YF-16 in the ACF 'fly-off'.

The stakes were huge, for the winner of the contest might remain in production beyond the end of the century. In addition to the USAF's need for no fewer than

▲ Connected to mobile 'huffer' carts to provide it with external power, YF-17 72-01569 undergoes last minute checks at Edwards Air Force Base prior to performing its maiden flight. (via Philip Jarrett)

The YF-17 was a real high performer for it wasn't burdened down with any of the systems that go into an operational fighter. It was a no-frills ship and it was *fast*. It was like driving a race car instead of your Chevy.

Capt Lonny K McClung
US Navy Test Pilot
Edwards AFB, 1976

1400 aeroplanes, the fighter chosen for production would also be selected for the 'deal of the century' under which NATO nations would order a minimum of 348 fighters to replace the Lockheed F-104 Starfighter from the late 1970s. It was also assumed that Australia, Canada, Japan and other countries would select the ACF. 'Sell the YF-17 to the USAF', Northrop's personnel were told, 'and you'll have a job for all the remaining years of your working life'.

On 13 January 1975, after months of head-to-head competition between the YF-16 and the YF-17, Air Force Secretary Dr John L McLucas announced that the General Dynamics fighter had triumphed. The Northrop design had lost due to its poorer range and greater cost. The price advantage enjoyed by the YF-16 stemmed

from the fact that the aircraft used a proven engine that was already in production for the F-15. Ultimately, the USAF felt that the F-16 Fighting Falcon was best able to move from technology demonstrator to production fighter.

The YF-17 might have died a death there but for the fact that the US Navy was now keen to obtain a new fighter also. Like the USAF with the F-15, the high cost of the F-14 Tomcat had prompted the US Navy to look for a less expensive type to serve alongside it. From 1971, the study into such a machine was broadened so that any such LWF should also have a secondary attack capability – this became known as the fighter-attack experimental (VFAX). The US Navy wanted an all-new design to fulfil this requirement, but the US Congress instructed it to take a close look at the USAF's ACF contenders. In late August 1974 the VFAX operational requirements were issued, and Northrop teamed up with experienced naval aircraft manufacturer McDonnell Douglas to promote the YF-17. General Dynamics joined with Long-Temco-Vought to meet the demand.

Evaluation of the two contenders was primarily a paper exercise that ended on 2 May 1975 when the US Navy selected McDonnell Douglas/Northrop's aircraft, now designated the F/A-18. The latter was chosen principally because it boasted two engines – a must for over-water operations due to the flight safety advantages that two engines have over a single powerplant. The F/A-18 also offered better multi-mission capability as well as superior maintainability on the flightdeck of an aircraft carrier.

Despite winning the VFAX competition, much work lay ahead for Northrop and McDonnell Douglas as they transformed the prototype YF-17 into a frontline, carrier-capable light strike fighter in the form of the F/A-18. In order to achieve this, the aircraft grew steadily heavier, larger in size and more costly. Many of the changes incorporated into the jet arose from US Navy requirements while others were the direct result of the fighter being 'navalised'.

Although selected by the US Navy in May 1975, redesigning the aircraft kept both companies busy until year-end. Indeed, it was not until 22 January 1976 that McDonnell Douglas received a written contract for an initial batch of 11 jets for full-scale development (FSD) testing. Nine of these would be completed as single-seat F/A-18As and two would be two-seat TF-18As (later redesignated F/A-18Bs). The maiden flight for the first of these aircraft was set for July 1978.

Having received the contract to build 11 FSD airframes, Northrop and McDonnell Douglas set about turning the YF-17 into the F/A-18 – this designation was not officially adopted by the US Department of Defense until 1 April 1984, although the aircraft was referred to as the F/A-18 from 1980. One of the main engineering issues to be resolved in this process was how to make the airframe capable of withstanding a 24-feet-per-second descent rate synonymous with carrier landings. In an effort to increase stability during carrier landings on a pitching deck, the aircraft's main landing gear was moved further aft, and given an 'L' shape instead of the original vertical design. The undercarriage was also considerably strengthened to cope with the rigours of deck operations. A twin-wheel design incorporating a forward launch bar was adopted for the nose landing gear, and it was configured to retract forward into the nose section.

The fuselage spine was enlarged, while the width of the aft area was increased by four inches. The jet's internal fuel capacity was also made considerably larger, from 5500lbs to 10,800lbs. The Hornet's wing area was increased from 350 square feet

◀ The first F-18A (BuNo 160775) takes off from Lambert-St Louis Airport on 18 November 1978 at the start of its maiden flight. McDonnell Douglas Chief Test Pilot 'Jack' Krings was at the controls, and he was chased by an F-4 and an F-15 throughout the 50-minute flight. (Boeing)

Did you know?
The seven-year
contract signed by
McDonnell Douglas
and Northrop with
the Department of
Defense covering
the production of
11 FSD research and
development aircraft
on 22 January 1976
was valued at
$1.43 billion.

with the YF-17 to 400 square feet, and they were two feet greater in span. Chord was also raised to 20 degrees to improve handling characteristics at slower speeds. The aircraft's stabilators were also enlarged, while the vertical fins were canted outwards at 20 degrees, rather than 18 degrees as seen on the YF-17.

One of the most important changes was the replacement of the YF-17's Westinghouse radar, which had limited range due to the aircraft being originally built purely as a close range air-to-air fighter. The US Navy insisted that the jet had to be capable of firing radar-guided AIM-7 Sparrow air-to-air missiles up to a distance of 30 nautical miles. In order to achieve this McDonnell Douglas chose the Hughes AN/APG-65 digital multi-mode pulse-Doppler 'look-down, shoot-down' radar for fitment in the Hornet. A 28-inch radar dish was required to meet the US Navy's weapons system search range requirement, and this could only be housed within the nose of the aircraft if the diameter of the radome was enlarged by four inches. The cockpit of the fighter was also moved back four inches.

The compact AN/APG-65 proved to be just as adept in the air-to-ground role as it was in air-to-air mode. This in turn meant that separate fighter (F-18) and attack (A-18) versions of the aircraft no longer needed to be built – the US Navy had initially planned to buy 780 Hornets (as the aircraft was christened on 1 March 1977), half of them fighters and the remainder optimised for ground attack. One aircraft could now perform both missions without the need for significant systems changes

former manufactured the wings, stabilators and forward fuselage, while Northrop built the centre and aft fuselage sections and the vertical stabilisers. These were then shipped to McDonnell Douglas' plant in St Louis, Missouri, where they were mated with the wings and forward fuselage. Flight testing was also conducted from here. The extra 20 per cent of the work undertaken by McDonnell Douglas covered the final assembly of the aircraft.

The first FSD Hornet was rolled out of the St Louis facility on 13 September 1978 and made its maiden flight, with McDonnell Douglas chief test pilot John E 'Jack' Krings at the controls, on 18 November. He was airborne for 50 minutes, during which time the jet reached a top speed of 300 knots and an altitude of 24,000 ft. As with most US military aircraft, the

that would have previously required the swapping out of a few 'black boxes' on the ground. The pilot simply had to switch the AN/APG-65 from air-to-air to air-to-ground mode.

When it came to constructing the FSD jets (and production F/A-18s for that matter), McDonnell Douglas and Northrop would adopt a 60/40 workshare spilt. The

◀ FSD 2 (BuNo 160776), which flew for the first time on 12 March 1979, undertook much of the propulsion and flight performance testing for the Hornet from NATC Patuxent River. Retired from service following the completion of Hornet flight trials in the early 1980s, this aircraft eventually ended up being used as a training airframe for Crash and Salvage Division personnel aboard USS Harry S Truman (CVN-75). (via Philip Jarrett)

majority of the Hornet flight testing was undertaken at the parent service's main test site – in this case Naval Air Test Center Patuxent River, Maryland. The first FSD jet arrived here January 1979, and it was joined by the second airframe two months later. All 11 FSD Hornets had flown by March 1980, and they would subsequently complete 2756 test flights totalling 3583 hours. With the F/A-18 sharing a similar configuration to the YF-17, which had undergone exhaustive testing (including 5000 wind tunnel hours) during the LWF competition, both the manufacturers and the US Navy hoped that the Hornet's flight test phase would proceed smoothly. However, myriad problems soon arose, the most serious of which could only be cured through the partial redesign of the wing and tail section.

The most serious deficiencies highlighted during the test phase were the Hornet's poor range and slow roll rate. The latter was caused by the flexing of the outer wing sections in high load situations and Sidewinder missiles, when fitted to the wingtip stations, causing too much roll dampening. Strengthening the wing spar and removing the dogtooth on the leading-edge of the wing flap cured the flexing issue. The ailerons were also extended and the leading-edge flaps split. Wing rigidity was improved through the thickening of composite skins. Finally, the wingtip launcher rails were moved forward by five inches and angled to a sharper nose-down incidence.

The range problem proved more difficult to solve, and it still remains an issue to this day. US Navy requirements had stated that the Hornet must have a range of 444 nautical miles when configured as a fighter and 635 nautical miles when being used as an attack aircraft. Initial tests at Patuxent River resulted in figures of 400 and 580 nautical miles, respectively. Critics of the aircraft were quick to highlight this deficiency, with veteran *Washington Post* investigative reporter Jack Anderson commenting that the Hornet 'uses too much fuel to be a good attack plane. To make it back to base, it must climb to fuel-conserving high altitude immediately after attacking its target, making it vulnerable to enemy detection and counterattack'.

The range issue came to a head in 1982 when test and evaluation squadron VX-5 published a report that cited the Hornet's shortcomings as a direct replacement for the A-7E Corsair II. The US Navy countered this by claiming that the test results were based on faulty mission profiles. Indeed, one official stated, 'The aircraft are different. If you force the F/A-18 to fly the same profiles that are optimum for the A-7 it will perform badly. However, the F/A-18 does as well or better when flown properly.'

Did you know?
When the prototype Hornet made its first flight from Lambert-St Louis Airport on 18 November 1978 in the hands of McDonnell Douglas chief test pilot 'Jack' Krings, it was accompanied by an F-4 Phantom II and F-15 Eagle acting as chase aircraft.

More problems arose when the first FSD Hornets completed the aircraft's first carrier qualification period aboard USS *America* (CV-66) from 30 October to 3 November 1979. In the lead up to the embark, FSD aircraft No 3 had undertaken 70 land catapult launches and 120 arrested landings at Patuxent River, and once operating from CV-66 off the Atlantic coast it tallied a further 32 arrested recoveries. Although the aircraft performed well – the pilots involved caught the targeted third wire 24 times – the jet's landing approach speed was alarmingly high. The US Navy had stipulated a 115- to 125-knot approach speed with no wind over the flightdeck, but the FSD aircraft had failed to get below

◄ *An F-4S from Fleet Replacement Squadron VF-171 shares deck space with FSD 3 aboard USS* America *(CV-66) during the Hornet's first carrier qualification period. This ran from 30 October to 3 November 1979, with CV-66 sailing off the coast of Virginia. Also flying from USS* John F Kennedy *(CV-67) and USS* Carl Vinson *(CVN-70), FSD 3 was subsequently written off in a hard landing at Pax River on 16 March 1981. (Boeing)*

140 knots. The solution to this problem was the reconfiguring of the leading-edge flaps 30 degrees and the trailing-edge flaps to 45 degrees of depression. The aircraft's flight control software was also modified, and a combination of the two brought the approach speed down to a more acceptable 134 knots. By the time the first production standard F/A-18s began to reach the US Navy in February 1981, virtually all of the deficiencies raised by the FSD test programme had been rectified and modifications incorporated into aircraft destined for frontline use.

▲ *FSD 5 (BuNo 160779) flies in formation with a development YF-15A assigned to McDonnell Douglas. This Hornet had a full avionics and weapons system fit, and was used in many of the early missile-firing trials. (Boeing)*

CONSTRUCTION AND POWERPLANT

Although the Hornet embodied many of the latest advances in fighter design, including the use of composite materials, most aspects of the airframe were well proven by the time the first FSD aircraft were built. Just under half (49.6 per cent) of its structural weight was made up of aluminium, with steel contributing a further 16.7 per cent. Titanium added a further 12.9 per cent – most notably for wing, fin and horizontal tail attachments, as well as for the wing-fold joints. Despite covering close to 40 per cent of the surface area, strong, corrosion resistant advanced graphite/epoxy composite material accounted for just 9.9 per cent of the weight, with the remaining 10.0 per cent being made up of other materials.

◄ Late-build F/A-18A/Bs near completion in the McDonnell Douglas plant in St Louis in the mid-1980s. Behind them are F-15Cs and a solitary AV-8B. The Hornet was in production with McDonnell Douglas from 1977 through to 2000. (Boeing)

Beneath the skin, the fuselage is essentially a semi-monocoque structure consisting of three major sections. These are primarily fabricated from light alloy, with machined aluminium fuselage frames and titanium firewalls between the twin F404 engines. The main undercarriage is also stowed within the central fuselage, with the nose gear retracting forward into a bay beneath the cockpit. The engine air intakes are also centrally mounted.

The aircraft's wing is very much a Northrop product, having a trapezoidal planform and incorporating variable camber – both Northrop traits previously seen in the company's F-5 family of fighters. Of cantilever construction, and made up of light alloy and graphite/epoxy composite, it has a six-spar machined aluminium alloy torsion box at its heart. The wing's most

Did you know?

Of the Hornet's 268 access panels, 238 of them can be reached by a man standing on the ground. Some 53 per cent are fitted with quick-release latches, while most of the others have only three or four fasteners to give quick access to aircraft systems and avionics. By comparison, most access panels for the F-14 Tomcat had more than 30 fasteners to keep them in place!

novel features are the LEXs, which extends forward on either side of the fuselage to a point that is adjacent to the front of the cockpit. The combination of the trapezoidal wing and the LEXs make the Hornet highly manoeuvrable in subsonic flight and capable of sustained controlled flight at high angles-of-attack.

The wing boasts full-span leading-edge flaps and hydraulically operated single-slotted trailing-edge flaps. The management

optimum performance. The fully-variable horizontal tailplanes are also hydraulically operated, and they can be used for both pitch and roll control. Constructed in a similar way to the wing and tailplanes, the Hornet's distinctive twin vertical tails were adopted by Northrop in the YF-17 project in an effort to offset the vortex flows created by the LEXs. They are mounted as far forward as possible so as to close the aerodynamic gap between the trailing-edge of their extension and retraction is done of the wing and the leading-edge of the by the aircraft's flight systems computer, vertical tail. The location of the tails results which sets the most effective angle to give in smooth and drag-free fuselage airflow.

The fins were initially attached to the fuselage with six attachment frames, but fatigue in this area prompted all Hornets to be grounded in 1984 when it was discovered that turbulent air from the LEXs was making the fin tips 'flutter' in flight. The severity of the lateral movement caused fatigue-induced cracks, which had to be repaired at McDonnell Douglas' expense.

Did you know?

The Hornet's outer wing panels can be folded upwards through 100 degrees at the inboard edge of each aileron so as to facilitate stowage on a crowded carrier flightdeck and to allow the aircraft to use small deck lifts. The wings fold under power, supplied by AiResearch mechanical drive.

This problem was fixed by 'beefing up' the fin-to-fuselage attachment points through the fitment of three stiffeners (called 'doublers' by the manufacturer) per fin.

Beneath the skin, the F/A-18 became the first production aircraft to boast a quadruple digital fly-by-wire control system. In layman's terms, 'stick and rudder' inputs are noted by a computer which in turn issues the desired commands to the jet's various control surfaces, while at the same time not allowing the pilot to overstress the airframe.

General Electric is responsible for Hornet propulsion, its afterburner-augmented F404 low-bypass turbofan engine being developed concurrently with the P-530 Cobra. Originating as the GE 15 in the late 1960s, it flew for the first time as the YJ101 in the YF-17 in June 1974. In its production form as the F404-GE-400, the powerplant was broadly similar in layout to the YJ101 but some ten per cent larger in size.

Being relatively small, the engine has proven easy to maintain at sea aboard the cramped confines of an aircraft carrier. Indeed, the entire unit has been designed so that maintainers can lower it out of the belly of the jet.

Routine servicing has also been made much simpler through the fitment of an in-flight engine condition monitoring system. This checks engine performance electronically, alerting the pilot to any faults and creating a read-out for maintenance personnel. Although essentially an all-new engine, the F404 experienced few serious problems in service. One of its key attributes was its extreme resistance to compressor stalls, even at high angles of attack. Its responsiveness has also been

◄ The F/A-18A/B's General Electric F404-GE-400 low bypass turbofan engine, rated at 16,000 lb thrust. It was developed from the YJ101 engine fitted to the YF-17. In the late 1980s GE began marketing the F404-GE-402 Enhanced Performance Engine (EPE), and this was fitted to the F/A-18C/D. The US Navy planned to retrofit the EPE to its F/A-18A/Bs, but this programme was abandoned in the mid-1990s due to cost. (General Electric)

praised, the engine accelerating from idle to full afterburner in less than four seconds. However, specific fuel consumption and the time taken to accelerate the F/A-18 from Mach 0.8 to Mach 1.6 initially fell short of desired levels. These were rectified with later versions of the F404. In its original form, the J101 developed some 15,000lbs of thrust, and by the time it had been developed into the F404 this figure had been increased to 16,000lbs.

The engines fitted in a Hornet are identical, easing maintenance and spares problems. Located side-by-side in the rear fuselage engine bay, they are toed out slightly so that the intakes are much farther apart than the variable area afterburner nozzles. A total of 11,000lbs of JP-4 or JP-5 fuel for the F404s is contained within six self-sealing, foam-protected tanks. The entire fuel system is carefully designed to minimise fire risk. Typically, the Hornet will always fly with external fuel tanks, up to three of which can be fitted. In the latter configuration (two tanks is usually the norm, however), the single-seat F/A-18 has a maximum fuel load of around 17,800lbs.

The first production F/A-18A made its maiden flight from St Louis on 12 April 1980, and following formal acceptance checks it was handed over to the US Navy in May. Early aircraft were issued to test and evaluation units VX-4 and VX-5, where they were flown alongside FSD jets. On 13 November the first F/A-18 Fleet Readiness Squadron (FRS) was commissioned at NAS Lemoore, California, this facility being home to Light Attack Wing Pacific's 11 A-7E-equipped units at the time. VFA-125 'Rough Raiders' would have to wait a further five months before it received its first aircraft – from VX-4 – in the shape of FSD Hornet No 11. Two more FSD jets arrived in subsequent months.

Production aircraft finally reached Lemoore in September 1981, including the first F/A-18Bs (39 would be built for the US Navy), as the two-seat TF-18A had been re-designated the previous year. By year-end VFA-125 had nine aircraft on strength, allowing the training of instructors and the preparation of the syllabus to begin in earnest. With VFA-125 then being charged with supplying

▶ Early-delivery F/A-18A BuNo 161250 has its engines tested on the NAS Lemoore ramp during the spring of 1982. This aircraft was one of the first Hornets to be supplied to the Fleet Replacement Squadron, and it was used by instructors in their conversion onto the jet and in the preparation of the VFA-125 training syllabus. This aircraft was subsequently supplied to NASA in October 1987. (US Navy via Peter Mersky)

capabilities in air combat manoeuvring (ACM) against TA-4Js of VA-127, F-5Es of the Naval Fighter Weapons School and F-14s of VF-124. In single- and multi-jet engagements against all three types, the Hornet more than held its own. Indeed, early F/A-18 instructor pilot Cdr (later Vice Admiral) Dennis McGinn recalled 'We suddenly discovered that we were beating the pants off of everything else in the sky.'

Did you know?

Many of the US Navy's first Hornet pilots came from the A-7 Corsair II light strike community. These Naval Aviators had loved the homely looking 'SLUF' for its precision weapons delivery, yet they were totally amazed that this standard of accuracy was far exceeded in the Hornet.

◄ *Toting three 315-US gal fuel tanks, four 1000-lb iron bombs, two AIM-9L Sidewinders and a pair of AIM-7M Sparrows, this brand new F/A-18B awaits its crew prior to undertaking a photo sortie for McDonnell Douglas in December 1982. (US Navy via Peter Mersky)*

both US Navy and Marine Corps units with pilots and maintainers, it was manned from the start as a joint service squadron. This meant having equal numbers of men from each service on the staff.

VFA-125 sent some early detachments of aircraft to other bases (including MCAS Yuma, in Arizona, and NAS Miramar, in California) on the west coast, where instructor pilots explored the Hornet's

These early ACM sessions had shown that the Hornet was a real 'hot rod', especially when compared to its predecessor, the Corsair II. Instructors assigned to VFA-125 also raved about the new jet's cockpit Digital Display Indicators (DDIs) and hands-on-throttle-and-stick (HOTAS) controls, the latter allowing the pilot to control all instruments needed for air combat – weapons stores, weapons firing and radar acquisition – without having to look down into the cockpit. The DDIs and HOTAS provided sufficient workload reduction to allow a single-seat aircraft such as the F/A-18 to fly multi-mission operations that had previously been the domain of two-seat jets.

Despite these plus points in the Hornet programme, the operational evaluation (OpEval) of the F/A-18A by VX-4 and

◀ F/A-18A BuNo 161527 of VFA-125 and a TA-4J from VA-127 return to MCAS Yuma after completing an ACM sortie over nearby ranges. Both aircraft types featured heavily in the January 1982 deployment by VFA-125 to Yuma when the unit fleshed out its ACM syllabus. This particular Hornet was later passed on to the Blue Angels. (US Navy via Peter Mersky)

VX-5, which was completed in 1982, did not go quite as well. The aircraft missed the US Navy's range specification, fell short on between mission cycle (turnaround) times and had inadequate fuel reserves when returning to the carrier with ordnance due to maximum landing weight restrictions. Its flightdeck approach speed was also too high when carrying more than a minimal ordnance load. On a more positive note, the OpEval praised the F/A-18 for its 'bombing accuracy, radar performance and reliability (100 sorties without failure or maintenance), air combat capability and multi-role flexibility, overall reliability and maintainability, engine performance and aircraft availability'.

Nevertheless, VX-5 recommended that the F/A-18 programme be suspended until the range shortfall problems could be solved. McDonnell Douglas suggested

Did you know?

VFA-125 took a handful of early Hornets to MCAS Yuma in early 1982, where they conducted ACM with all manner of types, including the mighty F-14 Tomcat – then viewed as the best air-to-air fighter in the world. In a series of 34 close range air-to-air engagements between the Hornet and the Tomcat, the pilot of the F/A-18 was able to outmanoeuvre his adversary and get into position for a rear-hemisphere gun shot on 20 occasions. He also got close enough for a Sidewinder missile shot too. The Tomcat crew failed to achieve a single firing solution.

cures such as a thicker wing and an enlarged dorsal spine, but the US Navy rejected these and overruled VX-5's recommendations. Its carrier fleet was expanding and ageing F-4s and A-7s dating back to the Vietnam conflict urgently needed replacing. Cancelling or delaying Hornet production

would ultimately leave the US Navy short of modern aircraft, so the F/A-18A was cleared for service use without any attempt being made to solve the range issue.

By the summer of 1982 VFA-125's training programme was established enough to allow personnel from the first operational unit to arrive at Lemoore. VMFA-314, based at MCAS El Toro and formerly equipped with F-4N Phantom IIs, duly began the transition process on schedule in early August. During the early stages of the five-month course, instruction took place in the Hornet Learning Center, where pilots attended lectures on the aircraft and employed audio-visual equipment in order to familiarise themselves with the new type. Time was then spent in the part-task flight simulator trainer, which was a simplified Hornet cockpit that introduced the pilot to the HOTAS. This was followed by a spell in the operational flight simulator trainer, where the pilot could undertake a sortie from take-off to touchdown – either on land or from a carrier. The final simulator was the weapons tactics trainer, in which the novice would spend some 50 hours in total receiving advanced air-to-air radar training and basic ACM tuition.

Having passed the simulator phase of the syllabus, pilots were then allowed to fly the F/A-18. Around 70 sorties would be completed, these building on the areas explored by the pilot in the simulators. US Navy squadrons that followed VMFA-314 would subsequently complete an additional 20+ sorties getting their pilots carrier qualified (carqual) – VFA-125's instructor cadre had in fact still to undergo their first period of carqual operations when VMFA-314 arrived at Lemoore, this aspect of the training programme not taking place until September-October 1982.

Although Marine Corps units did not carqual in the early days of Hornet operations at Lemoore, their pilots did perform field carrier landing practice training on the base runways during the transition. VMFA-314 eventually went to

sea with the F/A-18 for the first time in July 1983, when it briefly embarked aboard USS *Constellation* (CV-64) as the vessel sailed off the coast of southern California. By then the unit had returned to El Toro from Lemoore, having been declared operational – despite possessing just five F/A-18As – on 7 January 1983.

▲ *VMFA-314 went to sea with the F/A-18 for the first time in July 1983, when it briefly embarked aboard USS Constellation (CV-64) as the vessel sailed off the coast of southern California. (via Philip Jarrett)*

VFA-25 was the second frontline unit in the US Navy to receive the F/A-18A, and it conducted work-ups with sister-squadron VFA-113 as part of CVW-14 aboard CV-64 in the spring of 1985. Here, BuNo 161955 is unchained prior to taxiing out at the start of a bombing mission in the SoCal Ops area off San Diego. Eventually passed on to the Blue Angels, this aircraft lost its nose radome when Hurricane Ivan hit NAS Pensacola in September 2004. It was subsequently stricken from service and retired to the National Museum of Naval Aviation on base. (US Navy via Peter Mersky)

That same month fellow 3rd Marine Air Wing unit VMFA-323 had taken VMFA-314's place at Lemoore as it commenced its transition from Phantom IIs to Hornets. It was declared operational by mid-1983, with VMFA-531 (also a former user of the F-4N at El Toro) then checking into VFA-125. The 'Rough Raiders' found themselves very busy at this time, as the unit also helped VFA-113 become the first operational squadron in the US Navy to switch from A-7Es to F/A-18As on 1 April 1983. Appropriately nicknamed the 'Stingers', the squadron received the first of its 12 Hornets on 16 August and had completed the transition by 25 November. The culmination of the training syllabus was an at-sea period aboard USS *Kitty Hawk* (CV-63) in mid-October. Setting a benchmark that future light strike units would try to emulate, VFA-113 tallied 260 arrested landings as it successfully completed all day and night carqual objectives.

The 'Stingers' deployed to MCAS Yuma, Arizona, in late November for three weeks of weapons and tactics training. Whilst here, the Hornet's remarkable reliability allowed VFA-113 to generate 30 per cent more sorties than had been planned for. Aside from dropping all manner of ordnance, the squadron also conducted ACM with TA-4Js, A-4Fs, F-4Ss and CF-5As. Detachments such as this would be routinely undertaken by other newly transitioned Hornet units throughout the second half of the 1980s.

Sister-squadron VFA-25 had received its first Hornet on 11 November 1983, just as VFA-113 was completing its transition. Regaining operational status in early 1984,

VFA-25 joined the 'Stingers' within CVW-14 and undertook the air wing's work-ups as it prepared for a Western Pacific (Westpac) and Indian Ocean cruise aboard CV-64. The carrier departed San Diego on 21 February 1985 for a six-month deployment. That same month two brand new units in the form of VFA-131 and VFA-132 completed their Hornet training at VFA-125 and transferred east to NAS Cecil Field, Florida, as the Atlantic Fleet's first two operational F/A-18 squadrons. By then VFA-106 was also up and running at Cecil Field as the Atlantic Fleet Hornet FRS, the unit being established on 27 April 1984. It would train up its first two squadrons (VMFA-115 and VFA-137) during the latter half of 1985.

In late August of that year VFA-25 and VFA-113 returned to Lemoore following the

Did you know?
The F/A-18 was derisively referred to as the lawn dart by some critics in its early years of fleet service, because 'when you threw one up, it came right back down'. This nickname was inspired by the F/A-18A's notoriously short range.

completion of the Hornet's first operational deployment. The cruise had been a successful one in terms of the number of missions flown by the 20 F/A-18As embarked, these jets accumulating more than 4200 flying hours and 2500 arrested landings (45 per cent of the latter at night) during the deployment. On a less positive note, the ongoing concerns about the jet's range had had a less than desirable impact on CV-64's cyclic operations. Because of limited deck space, an aircraft carrier usually operates to a launch/pull forward/land pull aft cycle, which means that its flightdeck is only available for landings every 90 minutes, except in an emergency. The Hornet's modest endurance in comparison with other aircraft in CVW-14 meant that a close eye had to be kept on the fuel states of the airborne F/A-18s and the availability of aerial tankers overhead the ship. The latter mission was flown by the KA-6Ds of VA-196, and according to an article published in *Armed Forces Journal* in April 1986, 'During the *Constellation's* first deployment with F/A-18s, somewhere between 70 per cent and 93 per cent of all A-6 sorties were flown for refuelling missions. Normally, only about one-third of all A-6 sorties are refuelling missions.'

Nevertheless, the US Navy pressed on with its conversion of A-7 units to the F/A-18, and in October 1985 the first Naval Air Reserve Force unit commenced its transition to the jet when VFA-303 was issued with the first of its ten Hornets at Lemoore. This moved signalled the end of reserve-manned units being seen as a repository for obsolete types no longer deemed suitable for frontline use. Eventually, ten US Navy and Marine Corps reserve units would be issued with the Hornet, although only a handful remain established in 2011.

The next air wing to deploy with the F/A-18 was CVW-13, embarked in the veteran aircraft carrier USS *Coral Sea* (CV-43). An Atlantic Fleet vessel of more modest dimensions compared with most of the US Navy's supercarriers, CV-43 spent much of 1985 conducting work-ups prior to deploying on 2 October. Unable to operate F-14 Tomcats from its flightdeck, the ship instead had no fewer than four Hornet units (sharing 48 jets) embarked. Two of these were VMFA-314 and VMFA-323, as Light Attack Wing Atlantic had just VFA-131 and VFA-132 operationally capable at this time. During the course of the Mediterranean cruise, CVW-13 would give the Hornet its combat debut, as detailed in the next chapter.

In February 1986 the US Navy announced that its prestigious Blue Angels flight demonstration squadron would be re-equipped with 11 Hornets at the end

An F/A-18A from VFA-132 is towed along the NAS Cecil Field ramp in February 1985. This unit had been established with the Hornet at NAS Lemoore in January 1984, and along with sister-squadron VFA-131 it participated in the first Atlantic Fleet deployment with the jet as part of CVW-13 embarked in USS Coral Sea *(CV-43). On 15 April 1986 three of VFA-132's aircraft took part in a HARM attack on Libyan targets in Benghazi, giving the Hornet its combat debut. (US Navy via Peter Mersky)*

➤ *The Blue Angels perform a flyby of USS* Enterprise *(CVN-65) off the Norfolk, Virginia, coast in April 1998. The team received its first F/A-18As in late 1986, most of the aircraft coming from VFA-125 – a number of the jets seen in this photograph were amongst those early airframes. (US Navy via Peter Mersky)*

of that year's display season, thus bringing to an end a 12-year relationship with the A-4 Skyhawk. Based at NAS Pensacola, Florida, the team was issued with early-build F/A-18As (and a solitary F/A-18B) that were no longer considered suitable for carrier operations. Each aircraft was fitted with a smoke generating system, new flight control system software optimised for aerobatics, new seat harnesses and a civilian instrument landing system and navigation equipment. The aircraft's 20mm

M61A1 Vulcan cannon and underwing stores pylons were also removed. Flying some 75 shows per year, the Blue Angels have displayed the Hornet across North America and the globe. Flying more than 34 F/A-18A/Bs over the years, the team transitioned to the F/A-18C in 2010.

▲ *The Blue Angels flew the F/A-18A from late 1986 through to the end of the 2009 airshow season, when sufficient surplus C-model jets were available for the team to convert. It retained the B-model Hornet, however, as there is a paucity of F/A-18Ds in the frontline. The Blue Angels used more than 34 F/A-18A/Bs during its 24 years equipped with the jet. (US Navy)*

CVW-13's *Coral Sea* deployment in 1985/86 initially followed the same pattern as countless Atlantic Fleet carrier cruises, with the vessel's battle group clearing the Straits of Gibraltar and sailing into the eastern Mediterranean. Exercises with NATO allies and port calls filled the first two months of the deployment, with the Hornet units acquitting themselves well against British Sea Harriers, Turkish F-4s and F-104s, French Crusaders, Mirages and Super Etendards and USAF F-16s. They also periodically intercepted Soviet long-range reconnaissance aircraft (Tu-95 'Bears' and Il-38 'Mays') as the latter attempted to over-fly the battle group.

In late January 1986 CV-43 commenced the first of four Freedom of Navigation exercises off the coast of Libya that saw the vessel cross the so-called 'Line of Death' established by Libyan leader Muammar Gaddafi. This line, drawn across the Gulf

◄ *With tensions running high in the eastern Mediterranean, the Hornet units were kept busy providing CAP for the* Coral Sea *battle group. In the early weeks of the deployment, all four squadrons intercepted Soviet Tu-95 'Bear' and Il-38 'May' long-range reconnaissance aircraft as they attempted to overfly CV-43. This F/A-18A from VMFA-314 is keeping a close watch on an Il-38. (US Navy via Peter Mersky)*

A second exercise involving CV-43 followed in mid-February, and this time Libyan fighters were more active in their sparring with Hornets from the ship. Pilots flying CAP missions had to keep a close eye on their erstwhile opponents due to

of Sidra, was in international waters, yet Gaddafi claimed that this was sovereign Libyan territory, and anyone crossing it would be attacked. This area became the scene of regular Sixth Fleet exercises, during which US Navy carrier-based fighter crews flying combat air patrols (CAPs) routinely found themselves intercepting, challenging and escorting Libyan air force MiG-23s, MiG-25s, Su-22s and Mirages.

◄ Libyan fighters were frequently intercepted, challenged and escorted by Hornets from CVW-13, this MiG-25P being engaged by a jet (BuNo 162416) from VMFA-314. As can be clearly seen, both aircraft are fully armed with live air-to-air missiles. This Hornet was sold to Spain in 1995, where it still flies today as C.15-75. (US Navy via Peter Mersky)

◄ The veteran carrier CV-43 had no fewer than 48 F/A-18As embarked when it departed on cruise on 2 October 1985, the aircraft being split evenly between two US Navy and two Marine Corps strike fighter units within CVW-13. (US Navy via Peter Mersky)

the unpredictability of some Libyan pilots, Hornets often being positioned just a few feet behind their adversaries, ready to shoot. Routinely the Libyan pilots did not even see the F/A-18s until they were 'in their six' (on their tail).

By late March USS *America* (CV-66) and USS *Saratoga* (CV-60) had joined CV-43 in Freedom of Navigation exercises. Early on the 24th of that month the cruiser USS *Ticonderoga* (CG-47) was sailing south of the 'Line of Death' when F-14As from VF-102 providing a CAP for its operations were fired at by Libyan SA-5 surface-to-air missiles (SAMs). US naval aircraft responded over the next 48 hours with a series of strikes (codenamed Operation *Prairie Fire*) on SAM sites and Libyan naval

vessels. Although not expending ordnance during these operations, Hornet units from CVW-13 conducted CAPs with F-14s from CVW-1 and CVW-17, although the Libyan air force remained on the ground. The carriers then departed the Gulf of Sidra.

However, on 5 April the La Belle discotheque in Berlin was bombed by Libyan embassy employees and three US servicemen were killed. Retaliatory strikes (known as Operation *El Dorado Canyon*) were immediately authorised by President Ronald Reagan, these taking place in the early hours of 15 April. Strike aircraft from CV-43 and CV-66 were involved, as were USAFE F-111Fs and EF-111s flying from

The pilot of VFA-131 jet 'Cat 104' sits patiently in the cockpit of his aircraft as it receives its final checks from squadron maintainers on the flightdeck of CV-43. Both Hornets are armed with AIM-9Ls, whilst 'Snake 406' is also carrying at least one AIM-7M. (US Navy)

bases in England. Army barracks, naval installations and Tripoli airport were all targeted, with 18 F/A-18As from all four units firing 30 AGM-88 high-speed anti-radiation missiles at various radar and SAM targets as they protected A-6Es from CVW-13. This strike gave both the jet and the AGM-88 their combat debuts. Numerous SAMs were fired at the Hornets as they attacked targets in Benghazi, prompting Commander Sixth Fleet, Adm Frank Kelso, to comment 'I don't think anybody else has ever flown a mission in any more dense a SAM environment.'

Other Hornets were assigned CAP for both carrier-based strike aircraft and the F-111s, although the Libyan air force again chose to stay firmly on the ground. According to VFA-132's cruise report, 'During the months preceding the March and April hostilities, more than 160 intercepts of Libyan aircraft had been successfully carried out by F/A-18s from *Coral Sea*. Because of the complete tactical domination of the these encounters by the Americans, the Libyan Arab Air Force wasn't home when our bombers paid Gadaffi a visit on 15 April.' Having been the only carrier to participate in every phase of the Libya operations in 1986, CV-43 returned home to Norfolk Naval Yard, Virginia, on 19 May 1986.

The last examples of 371 F/A-18As and 39 F/A-18Bs built for the US Navy/ Marine Corps were delivered by McDonnell Douglas in mid-1987. Later that same year the third Hornet FRS was established at El Toro in the form of VMFAT-101, whose job it was to train new Marine pilots and maintainers. Five more frontline US Navy units had also been re-equipped with the Hornet by then, three of them (VFA-151, VFA-192 and VFA-195) being forward deployed to CVW-5 at NAF Atsugi, Japan, following their conversion at Lemoore. A second reserve-manned unit in the form of VFA-305 had also started to receive Hornets in early 1987.

Although the Hornet's introduction to fleet service had been a successful one, the F/A-18A would only enjoy a relatively short first-line career in the US Navy. Indeed, by 1995 all bar one carrier-based unit had replaced its A-models with the significantly improved F/A-18C. Something of a 'Jack of all trades, master of none', the early Hornet struggled with limited range, poor bring-back capability and reduced weapons compatibility.

◀ One of the last US Navy units to receive brand new F/A-18As was VFA-15, based at NAS Cecil Field. The squadron accepted its first aircraft in October 1986 and commenced its maiden operational deployment with the Hornet – aboard the brand new USS Theodore Roosevelt (CVN-71) – on 30 December 1988. A McDonnell Douglas photographer took this formation shot of four spotless Hornets in June 1987. (US Navy via Peter Mersky)

➤ VMFAT-101 was the third, and last, F/A-18 Hornet FRS to be established, this unit being responsible for training Marine Corps pilots and WSOs at MCAS El Toro from October 1987. Amongst the first F/A-18Cs built, this particular aircraft (BuNo 163703) was issued new to VMFAT-101 in 1988. It is seen here dropping 1000-lb Mk 83 iron bombs on a range near Yuma. This aircraft presently serves with the Naval Strike and Air Warfare Center (NSAWC) at NAS Fallon. (US Marine Corps via Peter Mersky)

The C-model Hornet is much better than the F/A-18A from a functionality perspective, which allows the AN/APG-65 radar to perform more effectively with newer weapons such as the AMRAAM air-to-air missile, laser-guided bombs and other precision-guided munitions.

Cdr Andy McCawley
Commanding Officer
VFA-113

The F/A-18A/B replacement began as an Engineering Change Proposal to make the Hornet compatible with a new ECM system and data link and the laser Maverick missile. A decision was made at this time to re-designate the aircraft the F/A-18C/D to facilitate logistical support in the fleet. Externally, the new version of the jet looked little different from the original Hornet models, but internally substantial upgrades were made to the aircraft's stores management and armament systems and mission computer. New antennas associated with an improved ECM fit were also installed externally, with blister fairings fitted to the trailing-edge of the vertical

tails, leading-edge of the LEXs and on the nose. Initial production jets were fitted with the same GE F404-GE-400 engines as used in the F/A-18A/B, although the more powerful F404-GE-402 EPE (Enhance Performance Engine) became standard from January 1991.

The first F/A-18C made its maiden flight from St Louis on 3 September 1987 and was delivered to Patuxent River 18 days later.

The first example to be formally delivered to the US Navy joined the Naval Weapons Center at NAS China Lake, California, on 23 September. The OPEVAL for the aircraft went smoothly, although fuel deficiencies were again highlighted. VFA-25 and VFA-113 became the first units to receive F/A-18Cs in June 1989, followed by numerous other squadrons at both Lemoore and Cecil Field. The first Marine Corps units

◄ VFA-83 received some of the first F/A-18Cs to reach the fleet when it transitioned from the Corsair II to the Hornet in 1987-88. This particular aircraft (BuNo 163455) is armed with AIM-9Ls on the wingtip pylon, a single AGM-88A HARM under each wing, AIM-7Ms on the engine intake pylons and a solitary Mk 20 Rockeye cluster bomb unit on the centreline. Such a load-out was dubbed a 'Wild Weasel' fit for SEAD missions. This aircraft was issued to the Blue Angels in 2010. (US Navy via Peter Mersky)

Did you know?

The F/A-18C/D airframe does not look too dissimilar to the A/B-model Hornet due to the fact that McDonnell Douglas ran into the hard limit on the jet's growth with the creation of the improved version of the strike fighter. Carrier approach speeds and range set a cap on the Hornet's maximum landing weight early on in the jet's production life.

issued with C-model jets were VMFA-212 and VMFA-232 in 1989, their conversion being handled by VMFAT-101.

A total of 137 baseline F/A-18Cs were built before production switched to the more capable Night Attack variant in November 1989. The key aspect of this upgrade was the converting of the cockpit instrumentation (MFDs and HUD) so that they could be used when the pilot was wearing night vision goggles. The pod-mounted night-capable AAR-50 Thermal Imaging Navigation Set was also mounted to the right fuselage stores station of the aircraft. Finally, the AN/AAS-38 NITE Hawk forward-looking infrared targeting pod gave the jet a self-designating capability for laser-guided weapons.

These system were also fitted to the F/A-18D, the first 31 of which were delivered to the US Navy in dual-control

trainer configuration. However, from late 1989 McDonnell Douglas switched to the all-weather attack aircraft version as ordered by the Marine Corps to replace its A-6Es. The rear cockpit of the jet had the control column and throttle controls removed, with the latter replaced by a weapon control stick for the weapons system officer. He would use this device for steering infrared and television-guided weapons onto their targets. The F/A-18D Night Attack retained

◀ An F/A-18D Night Attack Hornet of VMFA(AW)-242 unleashes a 5-in. Zuni white phosphorous rocket from an underwing LAU-10 pod during a live fire exercise over a Yuma range. The jet is carrying four pods, which is a typical fit for an F/A-18D assigned the FAC(A) mission. The rockets will be used to mark targets for other strike aircraft. (US Marine Corps via Peter Mersky)

Did you know?

The F/A-18's great rival, the F-16, has gained 20 per cent in thrust and weight during its development over the past three decades. The Hornet could not follow suit because any increase in empty weight reduced the already limited bring-back weight to the carrier. This has meant that major airframe changes have had to be avoided.

the full combat capability of the F/A-18C, but with six per cent less fuel. A total of 122 jets were built for the Marine Corps, with VMFA(AW)-121 being the first of six squadrons to receive them in May 1990.

A total of 22 US Navy and Marine Corps units had been equipped with the Hornet by early 1990, and production of the F/A-18C/D was in full swing. This would allow a further 17 fleet and reserve squadrons to switch to the aircraft over the next six years. The various upgrades to the Hornet during the 1990s and beyond are described in the Global War on Terror chapter.

◄ *An underside view of a VX-4 F/A-18C armed with ten AIM-120 AMRAAMs and two AIM-9Ms. After a long development period, the AIM-120 finally entered service with the US Navy in September 1993 when CVW-8's VFA-15 and VFA-87 were supplied with missiles. (US Navy via Peter Mersky)*

The Hornet had first seen action over Libya in April 1986, and almost five years would pass before the aircraft again got the chance to test its mettle in the crucible of combat. On 2 August 1990 more than 120,000 troops and 300 tanks of the Iraqi Republican Guard (IRG) crossed the border and advanced rapidly into Kuwait following a long-running dispute over $5.5 billion debts that the government of Saddam Hussein owed to its oil-rich neighbour. The latter country, along with other nations in the Middle East, had funded Iraq during its conflict with Iran. The invasion caught most of Kuwait's 30,000-man military, and the rest of the western world, by surprise. By 3 August Iraqi forces had taken up positions in much of Kuwait, and they began preparing defensive fortifications. That same day Saddam announced that Kuwait had become Iraq's 19th province, and his troops set about fortifying the Kuwait-Saudi border.

When the IRG seized Kuwait, they also took control of a quarter of the world's oil supply. Despite this, there was no significant military action undertaken by nearby countries to stop Iraq from moving further south. The Gulf Cooperative Council (GCC), made up of Saudi Arabia, Kuwait, Bahrain, Qatar, the United Arab Emirates and the Sultanate of Oman rushed military units to positions along the Saudi-Kuwait border, but these small forces would not have been able to stop any large Iraqi attack.

On 2 August US President George H W Bush signed an executive order declaring a national emergency. He also ordered US Central Command (CENTCOM) to prepare for the defence of Saudi Arabia and other nations in the region, and to

Did you know?
More than 190 Hornets from the US Navy and Marine Corps, as well as 30 CF-188s from Canadian Armed Forces, were committed to Operation *Desert Storm*.

Did you know?

Marine Corps Hornets flew more than 5100 sorties in *Desert Storm*, and although several jets were hit by flak and SAMs, none was lost in combat. Two F/A-18Cs from VMFA-212 were, however, lost in a mid-air collision over Kuwait on 8 March 1991 during a routine patrol – the pilots both ejected safely.

initiate planning to drive Iraqi units out of Kuwait. That same day the United Nations' Security Council passed Resolution 660, which condemned the invasion and called for an immediate Iraqi withdrawal. On 6 August Saudi King Fahad met with US Secretary of Defense Richard B Cheney and CENTCOM Commander-in-Chief, Gen Norman Schwarzkopf, and invited the USA and other nations to send military forces to the Kingdom in an operation that was codenamed *Desert Shield*. In the past, Saudi Arabia had not allowed foreign troops to be based on its soil unless the country was faced with a serious emergency.

The US Navy's first response to the presidential order was to send USS *Independence* (CV-62) into the Persian Gulf on 8 August. With CVW-14 embarked, CV-62 became the first American carrier to operate in the restricted waters of the Persian Gulf for many years. The previous day, USS *Dwight D Eisenhower* (CVN-69) transited the Suez Canal and entered the Red Sea, where it maintained a roving patrol until early the following month. The vessel had CVW-7 embarked, and like VFA-25 and VFA-113 aboard CV-62, the air wing's VFA-131 and VFA-136 were tasked with providing round-the-clock CAP for key Saudi installations. Of these four units,

VFA-131 and VFA-136 were still equipped with F/A-18As at this time.

CVN-69, which was preparing to return home at the end of a sixth-month Mediterranean and Persian Gulf deployment when Kuwait was invaded, had departed the future war zone by early September. CV-62 followed several months later, by which time three more aircraft carriers had taken up station in the area – this number had doubled by the time Operation *Desert Storm* commenced on 17 January 1991. The first vessel to arrive in the Red Sea on 22 August was USS *Saratoga* (CV-60), whose CVW-17 included F/A-18C-equipped VFA-81 and VFA-83. The next carrier to be assigned to *Desert Shield* was the veteran USS *Midway* (CV-41), which had been sent to the Persian Gulf from its homeport in Yokosuka, Japan,

in October. The carrier's CVW-5 included three F/A-18A units within its ranks, VFA-151, VFA-192 and VFA-195.

Ashore, the Marine Corps had sent no fewer than seven Hornet units to Sheikh Isa air base in Bahrain, VMFA-212, VMFA-232 and VMFA-235 flying F/A-18Cs and VMFA-314, VMFA-323 and VMFA-451 operating F/A-18As. The final Marine

▲ *VFA-83's F/A-18C 'Ram 305' comes under tension on waist catapult four aboard USS Saratoga (CV-60) prior to launching on a CAP along the Saudi-Iraqi border in December 1990. The carrier was on station in the Red Sea supporting Desert Shield from 22 August. (US Navy via Peter Mersky)*

Tailhook extended, F/A-18A BuNo 162901 from VFA-192 prepares to enter the marshalling stack overhead USS Midway (CV-41) following the completion of a Desert Shield CAP off the coast of Saudi Arabia. The aircraft is armed with two AIM-9Ms and a solitary AIM-7M. BuNo 162901 is currently an exhibit in the USS Midway Museum, having been displayed on the flightdeck of CV-41 in San Diego harbor since its retirement by VFC-13 in 2005. (US Navy via Peter Mersky)

Hornet unit to reach the region was VMFA(AW)-121, which flew to Bahrain in January, just weeks after it had achieved operational status with the F/A-18D. All the Hornets were controlled by Marine Air Group 11, and they were committed to the joint air effort alongside Coalition assets as part of the USAF component of US Central Command Air Forces.

With Saddam refusing to withdraw his troops from Kuwait, the Coalition launched Operation *Desert Storm* on 17 January 1991. By then USS *Theodore Roosevelt* (CVN-71) and USS *America* (CV-66) had also arrived in the Red Sea. Both carriers had Hornet units embarked with their air wings, CVW-8 aboard 'TR' controlling F/A-18A-equipped VFA-15 and VFA-87, while CVW-1's VFA-82 and VFA-86 were equipped with F/A-18Cs.

Lt Cdr Mark Fox of VFA-81 was one of two pilots from the unit to down a MiG-21 on 17 December 1991. He was part of a section of four jets en route to bomb airfield H3 in western Iraq when they were vectored onto enemy fighters by a patrolling E-2C from VAW-125. Twenty years later, now Vice Admiral Mark Fox commands Fifth Fleet. (US Navy via Peter Mersky)

F/A-18C BuNo 163508 of VFA-81 was used by Lt Cdr Mark Fox to down his MiG-21 on 17 January 1991. Seen here with a victory marking just above its nose modex, the aircraft has an identical weapons load-out to the one it was carrying on the MiG-killing mission. Photographed inbound to Iraq later in the war, the Hornet is holding station off the right wing of a Wisconsin Air National Guard KC-135A. In between the two aircraft is an F-14A+ from VF-103, which was also part of CVW-17 aboard CV-60. (US Navy via Peter Mersky)

Lt Nick Mongillo was the second pilot to claim a MiG-21, his victim being downed by an AIM-9M. He is seen here with the Hornet that he flew on this historic mission, F/A-18C BuNo 163502. Now Capt Nick Mongillo is presently commanding officer of the Pacific Missile Range Facility in Hawaii. (US Navy via Peter Mersky)

Four F/A-18Cs from VMFA-212 prepare to launch from Sheikh Isa air base, Bahrain, on a DCA CAP mission at the very start of Desert Storm. Hovering in the background is a lone Marine Corps CH-53D. (US Marine Corps via Peter Mersky)

Involved in airfield strikes on the opening day of the conflict, the carrier-based Hornets quickly proved the aircraft's strike-fighter capability when Lt Cdr Mark Fox and Lt Nick Mongillo of VFA-81 downed two Iraqi MiG-21s en route to bombing airfield H3 in western Iraq. Tragedy also befell the unit on this mission, however, when Lt Cdr Scott Speicher fell victim to a MiG-25.

US Navy Hornets flew a variety of missions during the 42-day conflict, with these being split between strike (36 per cent) general support (34 per cent), and fleet defence (30 per cent). Initially, units were flying strike escort and fleet defence, but these missions quickly tailed off once air superiority had been achieved. Ashore, Marine Corps units primarily flew close air support and kill box missions (84 per cent), followed by general support (16 per cent), as they prepared the battlefield for reoccupation of Kuwait. VMFA(AW)-121 was heavily tasked in the Forward Air Control (Airborne) role, identifying targets for other air assets such as the AV-8B and A-10.

A variety of ordnance was employed by the Hornet in the air-to-ground mission,

This is the first time to my knowledge that an aeroplane has scored an aerial kill while carrying four 2000-lb bombs, then continued on to hit the target. If the MiGs had gotten in behind us, we would have had no choice but to honour their threat. You can't do that with 8000 lbs of bombs. We would have had to jettison our ordnance to face them, and that would have served their purpose in stopping our strike. They failed – we succeeded.

Lt Cdr Mark Fox
VFA-81
USS Saratoga (CV-60)

▲ As the sole F/A-18D FAC/A unit in-theatre, VMFA(AW)-121 saw a considerable amount of action over Kuwait throughout the conflict. By war's end the squadron had completed an impressive 557 missions totalling 1655.5 flying hours. The unit remained in the region post-war, and this photograph was taken on a March 1991 patrol over the blazing oil wells that dotted Kuwait at this time. (US Marine Corps via Peter Mersky)

including Mk 80 series iron bombs, AGM-62 Walleye TV-guided glide bombs, AGM-65D Maverick and AGM-123 air-to-surface missiles, Mk 77 napalm canisters, CBU-72 cluster bomb units, AGM-45 Shrike and AGM-88 anti-radiation missiles, GBU-10, -12 and -16 laser-guided bombs and LAU-97 folding-finned aircraft rockets. Approximately 11,179 of the weapons delivered by the Hornet were unguided, with only 368 precision-guided munitions being expended. This was primarily because the F/A-18 lacked an organic laser designator. Indeed, there were only four AN/AAS-38 NITE Hawk pods available during the war, and all of these were allocated to VMFA(AW)-121.

By 28 February 1991, when the conflict came to an end, Hornet units had flown more than 11,000 combat sorties totalling 30,000 flight hours. A total of 5513 tons of ordnance had been delivered, with Hornets achieving a full mission capable rate of 90.4 per cent. Remarkably, no missions were missed due to maintenance problems, despite the jets' high usage rate. Five Hornets were lost in total, but only one of these was due to enemy action. A further eight were damaged, including at least one from VMFA-314 that was hit in the tail pipes by a shoulder-launched infrared-guided SAM – one of three Hornets struck

▲ An RAF Tornado F 3 and an F/A-18A (BuNo 163132) from VMFA-451 form up after returning from a CAP mission in the early stages of Desert Storm. The single-role F 3s flew fruitless four-hour CAP missions over northern Saudi Arabia until 8 March 1991, while the multi-role F/A-18s of VMFA-451 soon switched to the air-to-ground mission and saw plenty of action driving the Iraqi army out of Kuwait. (US Marine Corps)

by such weapons. Although the Coalition had succeeded in freeing Kuwait from Iraqi occupation, a belligerent Saddam Hussein remained in power in Baghdad. The Hornet would remain a familiar sight in the skies of southern Iraq for the next 20 years.

GULF PATROLS AND BALKANS BOMBER

Aside from brief campaigns in the Balkans (1995 and 1999), combat operations for F/A-18 units in the decade following *Desert Storm* predominantly took place from carriers sailing in the Northern Arabian Gulf (NAG). Following the freeing of Kuwait, a No-Fly Zone had been created over southern Iraq with United Nations' (UN) backing as Operation *Southern Watch* (OSW) on 26 August 1992 in order to protect Shi'ite Muslims from persecution by Saddam Hussein's regime. Joint Task Force-Southwest Asia, consisting of units from the United States, Britain, France and Saudi Arabia, was established on the same date to oversee the day-to-day running of OSW. The Hornet proved to

◀ *Having been involved in the very early stages of* Desert Shield *in August 1990, VFA-136 and CVW-7 returned to the theatre aboard USS* Dwight D Eisenhower *(CVN-69) in October 1991. By then the unit had swapped its basic F/A-18As for brand new F/A-18Cs, three of which are seen on patrol over the Persian Gulf in March 1992. (US Navy via Peter Mersky)*

be a primary asset in OSW, its swing-role fighter/bomber capability seeing the jet flying both CAP and strike sorties over southern Iraq.

Whilst these missions were being undertaken by light strike units flying from Fifth Fleet-assigned carriers in the NAG (Northern Arabian Gulf), back in the USA McDonnell Douglas was kept busy throughout the 1990s upgrading the F/A-18C/D. In 1991, the Litton AN/ASN-39 inertial navigation system was introduced, as was the more powerful F404-GE-402 EPE. This engine offered an additional ten per cent thrust over the -400 series turbofan it replaced. From mid-1993 onwards new ALE-47 chaff/flare dispensers and an upgraded ALR-47 radar warning receiver were fitted, and in May 1994 the AN/APG-65 radar was replaced by the AN/APG-73

in new-build aircraft. Based on the earlier system, the improved radar incorporated a new data processor, a new receiver module and a new power supply, all of which gave the AN/APG-73 improved performance and reliability. Upgrades towards the end of the 1990s made the aircraft compatible with new-generation precision-guided munitions such as the AGM-84 Standoff Land Attack Missile, uprated AGM-88 HARM, J-series Joint Stand-off Weapons and the revolutionary Joint Direct Attack Munitions (JDAM). The aircraft's AAS-38 NITE Hawk pod was also significantly upgraded through the addition of a laser target designator/ranger, allowing a Hornet so equipped to self-designate targets and deliver LGBs. Secure radios, GPS navigation sets, a new IFF system and satellite communication receiver capability were also installed.

Did you know?
In June 1995 the F/A-18 recorded its two millionth flight hour with the US Navy and Marine Corps. Some 80 Hornets had been lost in accidents by the time this figure was reached. This compared favourably with the F-14 (140) and the A-6 (110), both of which flew similar missions to the F/A-18.

With the bulk of these changes being internal, the outline of the F/A-18C/D barely altered throughout its production life. However, the 48 F/A-18Ds supplied to the Marine Corps with aerial reconnaissance capability looked significantly different. Based on work carried out by the manufacturer on a dedicated F/A-18R reconnaissance platform for the US Navy in the early 1980s, but then abandoned in favour of external pod-mounted sensors carried by the F-14, the 'photo-recce' F/A-18D had its M61A1 cannon replaced with a palletised electro-optical sensor suite that slotted into the space vacated by the gun. Controlled by the Weapons Systems Operator (WSO) in the back-seat, the equipment recorded images onto videotape.

As we stood ready to launch the first wave of F/A-18 Hornets from 'Big E' at the start of *Desert Fox*, I said a prayer for those that might not make it back. As I watched my pilot make his way to 'my' jet, side number AC 410, I tried to keep a smile on my face. I watched my bomb-laden jet's afterburners ignite on the catapult, feeling the rumble as it tore loose from the pointy end of the deck. I think the best moment or feeling I can remember is the overwhelming sense of relief I got upon hearing 'Next bird in, Four-One-Zero, Hornet' coming over the ship's 5MC loudspeaker system. Then I watched my pilot and my jet safely catch a wire. After taxiing in, the pilot jumped out of the cockpit, snapped a hand salute and said 'Job well done!' I couldn't have felt better.

*Aviation Structural Mechanic (Hydraulic) Airman
Apprentice Billy Fields
VFA-105
USS* Enterprise *(CVN-65)*

The aircraft could also carry a data link pod for real-time transmission of the sensor 'take', a Side-Looking Airborne Radar pod or the USAF-developed Advanced Tactical Airborne Reconnaissance System (ATARS). Like the cancelled F/A-18(R), the F/A-18D can have the gun fitted back in place in just a matter of a few hours.

The first modified Hornet was delivered in February 1992, and typically around four aircraft have the ATARS system fitted at any one time within a frontline squadron.

Production of the F/A-18C ended on 19 December 1998 when the US Navy accepted its 464th example, 581 aircraft having by then been built. Including Night Attack variants, 192 F/A-18Ds (the last of which was delivered to the Marine Corps' VMFA(AW)-121 on 25 August 2000) had also been constructed by McDonnell Douglas.

All of these improvements were put to the test during myriad carrier deployments in the 1990s, most of which saw vessels spending varying amounts of time in NAG performing patrols over southern Iraq. As part of OSW, US, British and French aircraft enforced the Security Council mandate that prevented the Iraqis from flying military aircraft or helicopters below the 32nd parallel – this was increased to the 33rd parallel in September 1996. Further restrictions, including the introduction of a No-Drive Zone in the south following Iraq's hasty mobilisation and deployment of forces along the Kuwait border in October 1994, were introduced several years later to stop both fixed and mobile SAM launchers being moved into the southern No-Fly Zone.

The US Navy's principal contribution to

OSW was the mighty carrier battle group, controlled by Fifth Fleet (which had been formed in July 1995) as part of the unified US Central Command (CENTCOM), which oversaw operations in the region. Typically, an aircraft carrier would be on station in the NAG at all times, vessels spending around three to four months of a standard six-month deployment committed to OSW. Ships from both the Atlantic and Pacific fleets took it in turns to 'stand the watch', sharing the policing duties in the No-Fly

Zone with USAF and RAF assets ashore at bases in Saudi Arabia, Kuwait, Oman and other allied countries in the region.

The Hornet was at the heart of the US Navy's OSW commitment right from the start, following on from its successful participation in *Desert Storm*. In the ten years that No-Fly Zone missions were flown over southern Iraq, the bulk of these sorties were performed by light strike squadrons from the Pacific and Atlantic Fleets, as well as the Marine Corps. The aircraft also evolved in that time from being essentially a fair weather fighter-bomber that relied primarily on 'dumb' ordnance to neutralise its targets, to a sophisticated all-weather strike platform capable of servicing a multitude of DMPIs (Designated Mean Point of Impact) in a single mission with GPS- and laser-guided weapons.

The Hornet's effectiveness as an air superiority fighter has also been improved against the backdrop of OSW following the introduction of the AIM-120 AMRAAM missile in the late 1990s. Finally, the jet's 'killer' role in the crucial Suppression of Enemy Air Defences (SEAD) mission was honed to an unprecedented level through the regular employment of the AGM-88 HARM and JSOW against AAA and SAM sites in OSW. Most missions were mundane and boring according to the naval aircrew that participated in these sorties. However, this all changed with the implementation of Operation *Desert Fox* on 16-17 December 1998, which saw the launching of a four-day aerial offensive ostensibly aimed at curbing Iraq's ability to produce Weapons of Mass Destruction (WMD). Although triggered

and the Special Republican Guard. The aircraft carriers USS *Enterprise* (CVN-65) and USS *Carl Vinson* (CVN-70) played a key role in *Desert Fox*, the vessels' CVW-3 (which included F/A-18C-equipped VFA-37 and VFA-105 and VMFA-312) and CVW-11 (with VFA-22 and VFA-94, again with F/A-18Cs, and VFA-97, equipped with the last F/A-18As in fleet service) flying more than 400 sorties in the 25+ strikes launched during the campaign.

Although *Desert Fox* lasted for just four days, its consequences were felt right up until OIF in March 2003. Proclaiming a victory after UN weapons inspectors had left Iraq on the eve of the bombing campaign, Saddam brazenly challenged patrolling ONW and OSW aircraft by moving mobile SAM batteries and AAA weapons into the exclusion zones. Both

◄ *VFA-37, which was part of CVW-3 aboard* USS Enterprise *(CVN-65), made history during Desert Fox when it sent female TACAIR pilots into combat for the very first time. Back from her mission on 17 December 1998, Lt Carol Watts conduct a traditional fighter pilot's debrief with Lt Lyndsi Bates in the VFA-37 ready room. (US Navy)*

by Saddam's unwillingness to co-operate with UN inspections of weapons sites, many observers believed that the primary aim of *Desert Fox* was to attack the Iraqi leadership in a series of decapitation strikes. To this end, a presidential palace just south of Baghdad was hit, as were buildings that housed the Special Security Organisation

were used in the coming months, and Iraqi combat aircraft also started to push more regularly into the No-Fly Zones.

In the post-Desert Fox world, these violations provoked a swift, but measured, response from JTF-SWA's Combined Air Operations Center (CAOC), which controlled the entire No-Fly Zone mission planning element, and created a daily Air Tasking Order (ATO) for all Coalition participants (both naval and shore-based aviation assets). Typically, such missions were devised within the CAOC-approved pre-planned retaliatory strike framework, and they soon became known as Response Options (ROs). The latter allowed No-Fly Zone enforcers to react to threats or incursions in a coordinated manner through the execution of agreed ROs against pre-determined targets such as

◀ In March 2000 VMFA(AW)-121 made history by becoming the first land-based Marine Corps Hornet unit to be assigned to OSW. Remaining in-theatre at Al Jaber, Kuwait, for three months, the squadron's F/A-18Ds performed a total of 287 sorties into southern Iraq. Armed with AIM-7Ms, AIM-120Cs and AIM-9Ms, this VMFA(AW)-121 section is conducting a DCA CAP over Iraq. (VMFA(AW)-121)

SAM and AAA sites and command and control nodes.

The level of conflict in the southern region in particular remained high into the new millennium, and between March 2000 and March 2001, Coalition aircraft were engaged more than 500 times by SAMs and AAA while flying some 10,000 sorties into Iraqi airspace. In response to this aggression, which had seen Coalition aircraft fired on 60 times since 1 January 2001, US and British strike aircraft dropped bombs on 38 occasions. The most comprehensive of these RO strikes (the biggest since *Desert Fox*) occurred on 16 February 2001 when CVW-3, operating from USS *Harry S Truman* (CVN-75), hit five command, control and communications sites.

Although the vast majority of Hornet OSW missions were undertaken by units flying carrier-based single-seat F/A-18Cs, in March 2000 F/A-18D-equipped VMFA(AW)-121 returned to the theatre for the first time since *Desert Storm*. One of the aircrew to participate in this unique deployment was WSO Capt Charles Dockery, who recalled:

We were in-country from March through to June. We flew all of our missions from Al Jaber, in Kuwait, having come into theatre to replace an Air Force A-10 unit. We were co-located with an Air Force F-16 squadron, so the whole set up of the operation was primarily USAF-driven. We were viewed by the CAOC as essentially A-10 replacements, but with a lot more capability to boot.

The unit was initially sent into Kuwait to simply perform the A-10's Combat Search And Rescue (CSAR) mission, but we also arrived with JSOW and JDAM capability, which was then very new in OSW. Indeed, the F-15Es and F-16Cs were not J-weapon capable at the time, meaning that the CAOC could only employ GPS-guided weapons when there was an aircraft carrier on-station in the NAG. We were able to fill in the gap when there was no battle group in the area. Therefore, although we primarily performed the CSAR role, we also tacked on the J-weapon precision bombing mission whenever we ventured into Iraq.

The next unit to deploy to Al Jaber as stand ins for the CSAR mission was VMFA(AW)-225, which arrived in-theatre in 2001. The last Marine Corps units committed to OSW were VMFA(AW)-332 and VMFA-212, which sent a composite detachment of six F/A-18Ds and six F/A-18Cs to Al Jaber from their forward-deployed base at Iwakuni, Japan, in April 2002. Both squadrons then rotated crews through the Kuwait detachment from their home base. This was the first, and only, time that such a deployment was handled this way.

The steady escalation of the conflict in the region was only brought to a halt, albeit temporarily, by the devastating attacks on the World Trade Center and the Pentagon on 11 September 2001. The subsequent declaration of the Global War on Terror by President George W Bush saw US carrier battle groups under Fifth Fleet control removed from their OSW station and pushed farther east to the Arabian Sea and Indian Ocean in order to support Operation *Enduring Freedom* (OEF) in Afghanistan.

The Hornet's key role in this conflict is detailed in the next chapter.

Although OSW was the dominant mission for Hornet units throughout the 1990s, the US Navy and Marine Corps also played their part in operations over Somalia in 1993 following the country's civil war, and in the Balkans in response to Serbia's aggression towards neighbouring Bosnia-Herzegovina and Kosovo. In April 1993, CVN-71's CVW-8 was involved in some of the first Operation *Deny Flight* CAPs over Srebrenica, VFA-15, VFA-87 and VMFA-312 flying numerous missions. VMFA(AW)-533 became the first land-based Marine Corps Hornet unit to be committed to this operation three months later when it sent eight jets to Aviano, in Italy, to serve under the command of NATO's 5th Allied Tactical Air Force.

➤ From April to September 1994 VMFA(AW)-224 deployed to Aviano, Italy, as part of the UN force for Operations Deny Flight and Provide Promise in Bosnia-Herzegovina. The squadron flew 1150 sorties for 3485 flight hours, a third of them at night. VMFA(AW)-224 deployed to Aviano once again in September 1995 as part of NATO Operations Deny Flight, Deliberate Force and Joint Endeavor. On 16 February 1997 the unit returned to Aviano for the last time, VMFA(AW)-225 participating in Operations Deliberate Guard and Silver Wake. (US Marine Corps via Peter Mersky)

All-weather strike-fighter units would continue to perform Balkan peacekeeping mission from Aviano for the next four years.

Marine Corps Hornets also patrolled the skies over the Adriatic, and on 11 April 1994 two F/A-18Cs from VMFA-251, again based at Aviano, attacked a Serbian T-55 tank and three armoured personnel carriers on the outskirts of the besieged town of Gorazde. On 21 November that same year F/A-18Ds from VMFA(AW)-332 targeted Udbina air base in Croatia, which had been used as a staging airfield for Serbian jets attacking Bosnia-Herzegovina. The Hornets led the strike, hitting SA-6 SAM sites with HARM missiles. The unit next saw action on 25 May 1995 when its jets struck weapons storage bunkers within a Serbian ammunition dump near Pale.

Three months later, on 28 August, NATO's patience with Serbia ran out when a shell was lobbed into a crowded market in the Bosnian city of Sarajevo, killing 37 civilians. Instigating Operation *Deliberate Force* later that same day, NATO strike aircraft flew hundreds of sorties against Serbian military positions surrounding key safe areas in Bosnia-Herzegovina through to 14 September. Again, Marine F/A-18Ds were in the thick of the action, VMFA(AW)-533 flying 180 sorties,

◀ *A Marine ordnanceman from VMFA(AW)-224 checks the fuse on a 1000-lb GBU-16 LGB at Aviano in April 1994 during Operation* Deny Flight. *The aircraft was also armed with an AGM-88 HARM, two AIM-9Ls and a solitary Mk 82 500-lb iron bomb. (US Marine Corps via Peter Mersky)*

primarily against the Serbian SAM sites. Many of these missions were flown at night due to poor weather during daylight hours preventing the use of LGBs from a safe height. Primarily employing GBU-16s, F/A-18D crews would fly at lower altitudes under the weather, relying on the cover of darkness to protect them from AAA.

Sailing in the Adriatic, CVN-71 committed CVW-8 to the operation, with its trio of F/A-18C-equipped units (VFA-15, VFA-87 and VMFA-312) flying SEAD and precision strike missions. Hornets also lased targets for F-14As from VF-41, the latter unit giving the Tomcat its operational debut as a bomber during *Deliberate Force*. On 8 September USS *America* (CV-66) arrived on station to relieve CVN-71, and the carrier's CVW-1 (which included F/A-18C-equipped VFA-82, VFA-86 and VMFA-251) flew strike missions alongside CVW-8 for the next four days until the latter departed for home. The concentrated application of air power eventually secured a ceasefire, and allowed a NATO force to enter the region to prevent the resumption of the fighting.

An uneasy peace lasted in the Balkans until 24 March 1999, when Serbian aggression against neighbouring Kosovo resulted in NATO launching Operation *Allied Force*. Again, Marine Corps F/A-18D units were at the forefront of the conflict, with VMFA(AW)-332 and VMFA(AW)-533 operating from Tuzla, in Hungary. Two jets assigned to the former unit were ATARS-equipped, despite the system still undergoing testing at the time. These aircraft flew more than 50 combined reconnaissance/strike missions, and the unit reported that the ATARS equipment worked well.

◄ During the 68 days of Operation Allied Force, VFA-87 expended 428,000 lbs of ordnance on targets in Kosovo and Bosnia. The unit was part of CVW-8 embarked in CVN-71, the carrier arriving on station in the eastern Mediterranean little more than a week after deploying from its Norfolk, Virginia, homeport. (US Navy)

Once again CVN-71 found itself in the thick of the action, arriving on station in the Adriatic just as *Allied Force* commenced. Its embarked CVW-8 included two Hornet units, VFA-15 and VFA-87, both of which were equipped with F/A-18Cs. By the time the conflict had ended in June, both squadrons had expended almost a million pounds of ordnance between them in just 68 days of fighting. Missions flown by the strike-fighter pilots included defensive counter-air, MiG sweeps, strike escort, SEAD and air wing alpha strikes. During the course of these missions, the Hornet proved its versatility by employing nearly every air-to-ground weapon in the inventory, including HARM, Maverick missiles, LGBs, iron bombs, Rockeye cluster bomb units, Walleyes and JSOW.

During the first week of the conflict, typically three large (18 to 24 aircraft) night strikes were flown every 24 hours, the Hornet units performing both SEAD and swing fighter-bomber roles within the strike package. As the war progressed and surface-to-air and air-to-air threats tailed off, two- and four-aeroplane self-escort strike packages became the norm as the air wing went in search of dispersed targets in Serbia and Kosovo. When operations shifted from fixed targets to Serb ground forces in Kosovo, the Hornet pilots worked closely with FAC(A) crews in F-14As from VF-14 and VF-41 – CVW-8's Tomcat units. Targets located would be marked for the F/A-18 pilots (usually flying in pairs) via the Tomcat's LANTIRN targeting pod, which was considerably more capable than the Hornet's NITE Hawk equivalent. By the time a ceasefire came into effect on 10 June 1999, the Hornet units in CVW-8 had flown more than 1800 sorties totalling in excess of 4000 flight hours. Squadron pilots had averaged 30 missions each in what had become the US Navy's longest air campaign since the Vietnam War. CVN-71 then headed to the NAG, where CVW-8 saw yet more action as OSW increased in its intensity. This would remain the case until 11 September 2001, as detailed in the next chapter.

Since September 2001, the Hornet has been at the forefront of the western world's global war on terror, seeing considerable action over Afghanistan and Iraq. F/A-18s were committed to this ongoing conflict just hours after al-Qaeda terrorists in hijacked airliners had attacked the 'twin towers' and the Pentagon. That morning, VFA-131 and VFA-136 were preparing to embark in USS *John F Kennedy* (CV-67) as part of CVW-7's cruise work-ups off the Virginia coast. North American Aerospace Defense Command (NORAD) contacted the US Navy soon after the south tower was hit and asked for its help in securing the airspace over

◄ With elements of CVW-7 (including Hornets from VFA-131 and VFA-136) hastily embarked, USS George Washington (CVN-73) patrols just off the coast of New York on the afternoon of 11 September 2001. The plume of smoke staining the horizon is from the 'twin towers' of the World Trade Center. (US Navy)

79

the eastern seaboard. Both CV-67 and USS *George Washington* (CVN-73) were put to sea by the Second Fleet, and the vessels embarked a handful of fighter squadrons from NAS Oceana.

VFA-131 and VFA-136 were sent to CVN-73, from where the units subsequently flew missions in support of the NORAD-controlled sea shield that had been hastily established off the coast of New York. The squadrons flew round-the-clock CAPs up and down the eastern seaboard. The skies remained eerily empty during this time, with all civilian air traffic having been grounded. After three days Second Fleet told CVW-73 to abandon these CAP missions and commence work-ups. Ashore, reserve-manned VMFA-321, based at NAF Andrews, Maryland, borrowed weapons from the USAF's 113th Fighter Wing and flew two CAP sorties over Washington, DC just hours after the Pentagon attack.

With al-Qaeda directly linked to the 11 September attacks, the US government turned its attention to the terrorist group's home in Afghanistan. Less than three weeks after the atrocities in New York City and Washington, DC, carrier-based aircraft would be in the vanguard of a joint operation to remove the Taleban from power and destroy the organisational infrastructure that al-Qaeda had established in Afghanistan.

The carrier closest to this land-locked country was USS *Enterprise* (CVN-65), with CVW-8 embarked. The vessel was nearing the end of a long deployment, and its air wing (including F/A-18C-equipped VFA-15 and VFA-87) had just completed five weeks of OSW patrols over Iraq when

the 'twin towers' were attacked. Also steaming towards the Arabian Sea from the Indian Ocean was USS *Carl Vinson* (CVN-70), with the F/A-18Cs of VFA-22 and VFA-94 and the F/A-18As of VFA-97 embarked as part of CVW-11. These five Hornet units, along with three Tomcat squadrons aboard both vessels, would be at the 'tip of the spear' in what was codenamed Operation *Enduring Freedom* (OEF) by Pentagon planners.

Sailing off the coast of Pakistan in the Northern Arabian Sea, both carriers were in position to commence strikes on al-Qaeda and Taleban targets by late September, although the first OEF mission was not generated until 8 October 2001. Politically prevented from using nearby land bases in

▲ VFA-94's 'colour jet' (BuNo 164066) heads up the 'boulevard' over western Pakistan towards Afghanistan on yet another OEF mission in October 2001. The aircraft carries a 2000-lb GBU-31(V)2/B JDAM beneath its port wing. Note the detailed mission tally to the right of the nose modex. (US Navy)

Providing round-the-clock air support for Coalition Special Operations Forces teams all over Afghanistan, many Naval Aviators logged a considerable amount of night flying in the early stages of OEF. (Jake Huber)

the NAG and India, and unwilling to over-use frontline airfields in Pakistan, Uzbekistan and Tajikistan, aircraft carriers were the only way initially open to the US military to bring tactical air power to bear in Afghanistan. The strike fighters of CVW-8 and CVW-11 duly hit terrorist training camps, Taleban barracks, air bases and SAM/AAA sites in the longest carrier-launched strikes in history. Hornet, Tomcat and Prowler units routinely

operated more than 1000 miles from their carriers in sorties that lasted between six and ten hours, traversing a route known as the 'Boulevard' over Pakistan in order to get to and from land-locked Afghanistan.

With no Coalition troops in-theatre to support during the early phase of OEF, the Hornet crews worked instead with two-man Special Operations Forces (SOF) teams, who sought out targets for the naval aviators to attack – they would also provide crews with target 'talk-ons'. Bringing the widest range of ordnance to bear (including LGBs, Maverick missiles, SLAM/ER – Standoff Land Attack Missile/Expanded Response – and JDAM, the latter being used by C-model jets only) of any tactical aircraft in-theatre, the Hornets was tasked with taking out fixed and mobile targets across Afghanistan. Known for its poor endurance, Hornets relied heavily on 'big wing' tanker support throughout OEF, with crews refuelling at least three times from USAF KC-10s and KC-135s and RAF VC10Ks and Tristars during the course of these marathon missions.

By the time CVN-65 was relieved by CVN-71 (with the F/A-18Cs of VFA-82, VFA-86 and VMFA-251 embarked as part of CVW-1) on 23 October, VFA-15 and VFA-87 had expended more than 450,000lbs of ordnance between them in just 15 days. Much of this had been dropped on targets lased by Tomcat FAC(A) crews from VF-14 and VF-41, using the LANTIRN pod. CVW-11's trio of Hornet units were also in the thick of the action during this period as well, as VFA-22's cruise report noted:

The initial days of OEF operations consisted of defensive counter-air and

high-value air asset protection missions over Afghanistan. In the second phase of the operation, VFA-22 flew strike missions and airborne interdiction missions. The third phase of the operation consisted of time-critical strikes and CAS, with much of the air-to-ground targeting provided on unusually short notice.

▲ An aviation ordnanceman assigned to VFA-22 attaches a fin to a laser-guided GBU-12 on an F/A-18C in preparation for afternoon flight operations from USS Carl Vinson (CVN-70) on 9 October 2001. (US Navy)

Flying air strikes into Afghanistan has proved a rewarding yet tiring task. The 2000-mile missions equate to flying from NAS Lemoore, California, to Tulsa, Oklahoma, and returning. The primary differences between the two routes is that the fine folks of Texas and Oklahoma won't shoot down a CVW-11 aircraft on the fly-over, not to mention the stress of a night carrier landing after six hours of flight time.

CVW-11 flight crews have set records for the longest combat flight in the history of each type of the air wing's aircraft. All three Hornet squadrons on board *Carl Vinson* flew more than 1000 hours during October. In VFA-22, every pilot from 'Rocket 1' to 'Rocket Last' logged green ink flying combat missions in-country. Squadron

pilots have employed a large number of laser-guided munitions and other types of smart weapons in combat. In October alone VFA-22 delivered nearly 200,000lbs of ordnance.

October had also seen the arrival of USS *Kitty Hawk* (CV-63) in the Northern Arabian Sea from Japan. However, rather than boasting CVW-5's full complement of aircraft, the vessel had only a small number of fixed wing aircraft aboard – three S-3B Vikings, two C-2A Greyhounds and eight F/A-18Cs. The veteran carrier's flightdeck was to be used as a floating Forward Operating Base for Special Operations Force helicopters instead. The Hornets (from VFA-192 and VFA-195) had been embarked to provide CAP for the ship, but they were soon attacking targets

in Afghanistan alongside other US Navy tactical fighters.

The F/A-18 units of CVW-1 and CVW-11 flew some of the most challenging missions of OEF as Taleban and al-Qaeda fighters fled east towards the Tora Bora cave complex and the Pakistani border. CVN-70 was eventually relieved by USS *John C Stennis* (CVN-74) on 15 December 2001, by which time its trio of embarked strike-fighter units had expended more than 1.2 million pounds of ordnance. CVN-71 and CVW-1 remained on station until early March, and the carrier's three Hornet units also tallied similar numbers to CVW-11's light strike squadrons in terms of weapons employed

and hours flown (the latter figure topped 9000). The F/A-18Cs of VFA-146, VFA-147 and VMFA-314 were embarked in CVN-74, and four days after the unit's arrival in-theatre the Tora Bora offensive ended. The fighting in Afghanistan then drastically reduced in its intensity, and things did not flare up again until early March 2002, when the US Army's Task Force Mountain launched Operation *Anaconda* in the mountains of eastern Afghanistan. Targeting 1000+ hardcore al-Qaeda fighters entrenched in ridgelines and caves throughout the Shar-i-Kot Valley, the offensive got badly bogged down to the point where the survival of US troops in contact with the enemy was only ensured through the overwhelming employment of tactical air power. During the final stages of *Anaconda* CVN-71 was finally relieved by CV-67, whose CVW-7 (including VFA-131 and VFA-136) flew its first missions on 11 March. In the following month six F/A-18Ds from VMFA(AW)-121 became the first aircraft to arrive at a newly established Coalition base in Kyrgyzstan, from where they flew missions over Afghanistan through to September.

By the autumn of 2002, the focus of the Global War on Terror had switched to Iraq, and as the call for regime change in the country increased, so did the commitment of carrier air power to Fifth Fleet. By mid-March 2003 no fewer than five aircraft carriers were within striking distance of targets in Iraq, three vessels – USS *Constellation* (CV-64), USS *Kitty Hawk* (CV-63) and USS *Abraham Lincoln* (CVN-72) – sailing in the NAG and two – USS *Theodore Roosevelt* (CVN-71) and USS *Harry S Truman* (CVN-75) – being

I was able to refine my aim point via the FLIR prior to visually breaking the target out of the blowing sand. The building began to take shape, and I was able to refine the aim point further still on my HUD before firing off 200 rounds and then conducting a max-G recovery manoeuvre. The explosive impacts of the 20 mm ammunition were visually significant enough to allow for corrections to the aim point, and the recorded FLIR imagery validated the hits on the sniper position in the fourth storey of the building. The Joint Terminal Attack Controller reported that firing from that position ceased after the strafing run.

Lt Cdr Spencer Abbot
VFA-37
USS *Harry S Truman* (CVN-75)

positioned in the eastern Mediterranean. Between them, the units could field 131 F/A-18Cs and 24 F/A-18A+s, the latter jets being flown by VMFA-115 and reserve-manned VFA-201.

The F/A-18A+ is a relatively rare aircraft in the US military inventory, with only 35 being delivered to the US Navy and 61 to the US Marine Corps in 2000–01. These jets had originally been issued to frontline units in the mid-1980s as Lot VII, VIII and IX A-model Hornets. Replaced in fleet service by F/A-18Cs and transferred to the US Navy and Marine Corps Reserve after less than a decade of frontline service, the airframes selected for upgrading to A+ specification in the late 1990s were chosen due to their low flying hours and carrier 'cat/trap' counts. They were upgraded to C-model avionics configuration, which in turn allowed them to use precision-guided munitions and AMRAAM.

Ashore, 60 F/A-18Cs and F/A-18Ds from the Marine Corps' 2nd and 3rd Marine Air Wings had been deployed to Al Jaber, in Kuwait, to provide air support for ground forces, including the 1st Marine Division and British troops, once the invasion of Iraq was launched. The two-seat Hornets of VMFA(AW)-121, VMFA(AW)-225 and VMFA(AW)-533 would be kept particularly busy performing FAC(A) duties for various Coalition strike aircraft.

Operation *Iraqi Freedom* commenced with the 'Shock and Awe' strikes on Baghdad on the night of 21-22 March 2003. CV-64's CVW-2 provided the lead Coalition force to hit targets in the Iraqi capital, its Hornet units (VFA-137, VFA-151 and VMFA-323) dropping JDAM and JSOW and firing SLAM ER and HARM. The F/A-18s also performed defensive counter air missions for other strike formations. Operating from Fifth Fleet's designated OIF night carrier, CVW-2 proceeded to fly the bulk of its missions masked by the

▲ Cdr Mark Hubbard, CO of VFA-151, poses for a self-portrait with his wingman during their flight back to USS Constellation *(CV-64)* during the 'Shock and Awe' phase of OIF. *(VFA-151)*

89

VFA-25's 'Fist 413' (F/A-18C BuNo 164266) launches from CVN-72 on yet another daylight mission to An Najaf towards the end of the 'Shock and Awe' phase of OIF. Thanks to the employment of precision-guided munitions by strike aircraft that enjoyed total air superiority over Iraq, the Coalition's aerial campaign against fixed targets had achieved its aims by 25 March 2003. (US Navy)

The Hornet squadron then switched to CAS strikes as the ground push towards Baghdad gained momentum in late March. The jet's ability to hit targets with all manner of precision ordnance in a timely fashion was greatly appreciated as Coalition forces engaged the Republican Guard around cities such as Karbala and An Nasiriyah.

F/A-18 squadrons in the NAG flew a broad mix of missions throughout the 28 days of OIF. VFA-25 and VFA-113 were flying from CVN-72, which was

cover of darkness. It initially used JDAM to hit fixed targets such as command and control nodes, SAM and radar sites, airfields and Republican Guard barracks, as well as presidential palaces and Ba'ath party buildings.

the designated day carrier. These units shared deck space with VFA-115, which was conducting the very first cruise with the F/A-18E Super Hornet as part of CVW-14. Operating the farthest north in the NAG was CV-64, whose CVW-5 included VFA-27, VFA-192 and VFA-195. The latter unit would suffer the light strike community's sole combat fatality in OIF when Lt Nathan White was shot down in error by a PAC-3 Patriot missile on the night of 2 April 2003.

The war waged by the two Mediterranean-based carriers contrasted markedly with that fought by the vessels sailing in the NAG. With Turkey having denied the US Army's 4th Infantry Division use of its territory as a jumping-off point, northern front activities centred on the support of SOF teams operating behind enemy lines. The teams relied heavily on CAS from CVW-3 and CVW-8, which were positioned in the eastern Mediterranean. Hornets from both air wings flew CAS missions for SOF units, often putting ordnance dangerously close to friendly forces. The support these aircraft provided undoubtedly saved the lives of Coalition

▲ Seconds away from launching off CV-63's waist cat three in the pre-dawn hours of 20 March 2003 – the eve of 'Shock and Awe' – VFA-27's 'Mace 206' (F/A-18C BuNo 164059) has a single GBU-12 attached to each outer wing pylon. (US Navy)

◢ JDAM and HARM sit side-by-side in the hangar bay of USS Abraham Lincoln (CVN-72) on 21 March 2003. These weapons were soon taken up to the flightdeck and loaded onto waiting Hornets, Tomcats and Prowlers, which expended them during CVW-14's first OIF strike. To the right of the photograph, in the second row, are at least six ADM-141C Improved Tactical Air-Launched Decoys. Used to simulate aircraft, these were also employed by Hornet units in the early stages of OIF. (US Navy)

forces on the ground, and eventually led to the capitulation of 100,000 Iraqi soldiers.

Prior to immersing itself in CAS missions with SOF, CVW-3's VFA-37, VFA-105 and VMFA-312 and CVW-8's VFA-15, VFA-87 and VFA-201 had completed a number of conventional strikes with JDAM and LGBs against fixed targets in Iraq. These missions, flown at the start of the conflict, were some of the longest of the war, covering distances of up to 800 miles each way. As the Hornet had proven in OEF, it

was more than capable of handling such sorties. Further strikes on fixed targets followed, with mission times being reduced slightly once Turkey permitted overflights.

CVW-3 was designated as the day carrier throughout OIF, whilst CVW-8 handled much of the night work. As the war progressed, CAS for SOF teams became the staple mission for both light strike units, and their success in this role was related by the commander of CVW-8, Capt David Newland: 'Dropping precision-guided ordnance for a SOF team was a mission

◄ *Armed with an AIM-7M training round attached to an underwing LAU-115 launcher, VFA-15's 'Valion 311' (F/A-18C BuNo 164680) departs CVN-71 via waist cat four on the eve of OIF. (US Navy)*

◄ *Tankers were as hard to come by in the north as they were in the south during OIF, and that was not good news if you were flying a typically fuel-critical Hornet somewhere over enemy territory. Sights such as this regularly greeted F/A-18 pilots as they rendezvoused with the duty KC-135s or KC-10s manning the three different tanker holding patterns, one of which was over Turkey and the remaining two over Iraq itself. All three of CVW-3's strike fighter units (VFA-37, VFA-105 and VMFA-115) have aircraft in the queue here waiting to top off their fuel tanks (Eric Jakubowski)*

➤ CVW-3's maintainers work through the hours of darkness readying aircraft for the following day's missions over northern Iraq. Here, aircraft handlers use a dedicated hangar tractor to move an F/A-18C from VFA-37 towards one of the deck elevators following the completion of rectification work aboard USS Harry S Truman (CVN-75). (US Navy)

➤ Topping off his tanks following his recent departure from CVN-75, the pilot of VFA-105's 'Canyon 410' holds his jet steady in the basket behind VS-22's S-3B 'Vidar 702' as both aircraft cruise over solid cloud. The first job for most Hornet pilots in OIF straight after launching would be to locate the duty Viking in the overhead above the carrier and take on 2000lbs of fuel to replace what had been used during take-off. (US Navy)

▲ Some 22 of the 36 F/A-18Cs assigned to CVW-2's trio of Hornet units during CV-64's OSW/OIF war cruise crowd Constellation's bow on 15 April 2003. VMFA-323 had dropped its final ordnance of OIF, near Tikrit, 24 hours earlier. (US Navy)

► The pilot of 'Canyon 400' (F/A-18C BuNo 164200) retracts his refuelling probe after topping off his fuel from an unidentified USAF tanker. The Hornet is armed with two 500lb GBU-12s and a single AGM-154A JSOW. By war's end this particular aircraft was VFA-105's leading JSOW dropper, its pilots having expended four AGM-154As. Eleven LGB and two JDAM symbols completed the jet's scoreboard, making it the unit's leading bomber (USAF)

▲ Looking every inch a war-weary warrior, VMFA-323's 'Snake 201' (F/A-18C BuNo 164722) patrols over Baghdad on the morning of 17 April 2003. The numerous bridges that cross the Tigris in the city can be clearly seen below the Hornet. (US Marine Corps)

The 19 pilots, 19 WSOs and 202 Marines and sailors of VMFA(AW)-242 enjoy a brief break from their punishing '24/7' flight operations schedule to pose for a photograph at Al Asad on 23 November 2004. Sat on the cockpit sills of the unit's colour jet are squadron CO, Lt Col 'Wolfy' liams (right), and XO, Lt Col Doug Pasnik. The maintenance personnel seen here were the unsung heroes of the deployment. (VMFA(AW)-242)

that gave immediate gratification. They were told where to aim the munitions, and they got direct feedback from the troops after they had expended their bombs.'

Although the occupation of Iraq had been successfully completed by mid-April, Coalition forces were targeted by suicide bombers and armed militants

Did you know?

Capt Mark Fox, who scored a victory over a MiG-21 with an F/A-18C on the first day of Operation *Desert Storm* on 17 January 1991, led the first manned strike on Baghdad during OIF on 21 March 2003. Commander of CVW-2 aboard CV-64, and flying a jet from VMFA-323, Fox received a Distinguished Flying Cross for his leadership of this mission.

during subsequent months. Things got progressively worse in 2004 as US and British troops struggled to keep a rising insurgency in check, and carrier-based Hornets remained a familiar sight in skies over Iraq through to early 2009. From August 2004, the Marine Corps also had a full squadron of F/A-18s in Iraq flying from Al Asad, a former MiG base. Operating closely with troops on the ground, the Hornets would be called in to target insurgents that had ambushed patrols or supply convoys. Pilots and WSOs would also scout highways ahead of Coalition forces in search of IEDs, the Hornet's effectiveness in this role being improved over the years through the fitment of the Multifunction Information Distribution System, Litening II (AT) FLIR targeting pod and ROVER real-time video uplink.

▶ 'Snake 201' (F/A-18C BuNo 164721) of VMFA-323 heads into Iraq on 20 March 2005, soon after the unit had arrived in the NAG with CVW-9 aboard CVN-70. This aircraft is equipped with one of just seven ATFLIR pods passed on to CVW-9 when CVW-3 departed the NAG. VMFA-323's CAG jet in OIF I, BuNo 164721 was written off in a mid-air collision with 'Snake 210' (BuNo 164732) over Iraq on 2 May 2005. Both pilots were killed in the accident (Guy Ravey)

▶ Seen on patrol from Al Asad over western Iraq in May 2006, VMFA(AW)-533's F/A-18D 'Profane 02' completes a mid-mission refuelling and heads back out towards the Anbar province. The jet is equipped with a Litening II (AT) FLIR (Forward Looking Infrared) targeting pod and a 500lb GBU-38 JDAM – the latter quickly became the weapon of choice in OIF II. (Doug Glover)

Did you know?

All frontline light strike Hornet squadrons had been reduced in strength from 12 to 10 jets each by 2010 due to an ever increasing number of F/A-18Cs being deemed unfit for carrier operations.

These assets proved invaluable in OEF too, with carrier air wings resuming operations over Afghanistan from September 2006 following a significant upsurge in Taleban activity on the country. The first vessel to answer the call of International Security and Assistance Forces (ISAF) in-theatre was USS *Enterprise* (CVN-65), whose CVW-1 strafed and bombed enemy positions. Thus began a routine of carrier-based strike-fighter missions in Afghanistan that continues to this day. Indeed, every air wing in the US Navy, bar forward-deployed CVW-5, has performed myriad OEF cruises over the past four years, during which Hornet units have provided CAS for ISAF troops on the ground.

▲ *F/A-18Cs from VFA-131 and VFA-83 are service and re-spotted on the flightdeck of USS Dwight D Eisenhower (CVN-69) following their return from an OEF mission on 18 February 2007. (Anthony Osborne)*

The 'colour jet' from VFA-192 launches from CV-63's waist catapult three in August 2005, the vessel sailing in the Pacific at the time. CVW-5 is the only air wing in the US Navy not to have been directly involved in either OEF or OIF since the liberation of Iraq in April 2003. (US Navy)

CVW-5's 'colour jets' have been consistently amongst the most garishly decorated aircraft in the fleet. VFA-192 and VFA-195 maintained this tradition with these two stunningly marked F/A-18Cs, seen here on a training mission over the Pacific in March 2008. (Katsuhiko Tokunaga)

An F/A-18C Hornet of VFA-136 tests its flare countermeasures system just prior to beginning a CAS mission in support of ground forces in Afghanistan on 7 November 2007. Assigned to CVW-1 and armed with three GBU-12s and a solitary Sidewinder, the jet was flying from USS Enterprise (CVN-65) at the time. (Pete Schue)

The VFA-195 'colour jet' takes on fuel from a KC-10 during Exercise Cope Tiger, held in Thailand in March 2009. As part of the forward-deployed CVW-5, this unit routinely exercised with various Asian allies both from CV-63 and shore bases. (Chris Hagstrom)

For several years OEF and OIF operations were running side by side, placing a great strain on Fifth Fleet assets. However, in the spring of 2008 CVN-72's CVW-2 became the last air wing to fly combat missions over Iraq. Similarly, the Marine Corps ended its unit rotation to Al Asad in January 2010 when reserve-manned VMFA-112 returned to the USA. Five months later, however, VMFA-232 deployed to Kandahar as part of the 3rd Marine Aircraft Wing (Forward) commitment to OEF. Seeing plenty of action whilst in Afghanistan, this unit was replaced in November 2010 by VMFA-122.

As this book is written, USS *George H W Bush* (CVN-77), with CVW-8 embarked, and USS *Ronald Reagan* (CVN-76) and CVW-14 are performing the OEF mission with Fifth Fleet, these air wings controlling four Hornet-equipped units between them.

◄ *VFA-136's 'colour jet' cruises over the Mediterranean Sea during a unit-level training mission on 21 July 2007. Embarked in CVN-65 with CVW-1, the squadron was heading for the northern Arabian Sea when this photograph was taken. (Pete Schue)*

◄ *Returning to CVN-65 following a training mission off the Virginia coast, this F/A-18C from VMFA-251 has 25lb blue training bombs attached to an underwing ejector rack. Such weapons duplicate the delivery ballistics of an LGB or JDAM when dropped, but cost only a fraction of the price of the real thing. (Pete Schue)*

VFA-86 served alongside VFA-136 and VMFA-251 as the third F/A-18C unit assigned to CVW-1 in 2006-07. During this time the air wing made two OIF/OEF deployments in the space of just 18 months. This aircraft is just seconds away from being launched off CVN-65's bow cat one at the start of an OIF mission in August 2007. (Pete Schue)

A very dusty 'Ragin 300' (F/A-18C BuNo 165176) of VFA-37 is guided onto CVN-75's bow cat one on 21 February 2008. Southern Iraq and the NAG are routinely plagued by huge dust storms during the spring. VFA-37 and the rest of CVW-3 were heavily involved in the pivotal Battle of Basra just weeks after this photograph was taken. (US Navy)

An F/A-18C from VMFA-312 closes on the stern of CVN-75 at the end of a training mission off the Virginia coast in April 2009. (Ted Carlson)

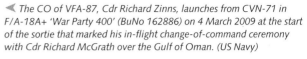
The CO of VFA-87, Cdr Richard Zinns, launches from CVN-71 in F/A-18A+ 'War Party 400' (BuNo 162886) on 4 March 2009 at the start of the sortie that marked his in-flight change-of-command ceremony with Cdr Richard McGrath over the Gulf of Oman. (US Navy)

◀ VFA-25's 'colour jet' (F/A-18C BuNo 164206) is carefully manoeuvred over bow cat two aboard USS Ronald Reagan (CVN-76) on 29 August 2009 during combat operations in the Gulf of Oman. (US Navy)

▲ Having just returned home to NAS Lemoore following a five-month Westpac/OEF surge cruise, six of VFA-25's Hornets sit idle on the ramp on 20 October 2009. Assigned to CVW-14, the unit undertook two operational deployments in the space of just 12 months in 2008-09. (Ashley Wallace)

VFA-25's sister Hornet squadron for the past 28 years has been VFA-113, whose 'colour jet' (BuNo 164668) is seen here heading for Afghanistan on 7 July 2009. This aircraft was destroyed by fire at Kandahar air base little more than a month after this photograph was taken. (Eric Etz)

Both equipped with Litening II (AT) FLIR targeting pods and 500lb GBU-12s, two VMFA-232 F/A-18Cs patrol over hazy Afghan skies in October 2010. Four months earlier, the unit had become the first Marine Corps Hornet squadron to deploy to Kandahar as part of the 3rd Marine Aircraft Wing (Forward) commitment to OEF. Seeing plenty of action whilst in Afghanistan, VMFA-232 was replaced by VMFA-122 in November 2010. (VMFA-232)

On short finals to the main runway at NAS Fallon, VFA-97's 'colour jet' (F/A-18C BuNo 164060) returns from an ACM hop over the instrumented weapons ranges that surround the naval air station. Note the orange AN/ASQ-40T large area training range pod on the Hornet's starboard wingtip. This photograph was taken during CVW-11's air wing Fallon detachment in April 2009. (James Dunn)

The Hornet has enjoyed only modest export success when compared to its great rival, the F-16. The first country to choose the F/A-18A/B was Canada, who believed that the jet's more reliable twin-engined design and better AN/APG-65 radar and avionics made the Hornet more desirable than the F-16A/B. On 10 April 1980 the Canadian government announced that it would purchase 114 single-seat CF-188s (later abbreviated to CF-18s) and 40 two-seat CF-118Bs (later abbreviated to CF-18Bs). Built to replace the veteran CF-101 Voodoo, CF-5A Freedom Fighter and CF-104 Starfighter, the Canadian Hornets were almost identical to the US Navy's F/A-18A/Bs. The first two aircraft were delivered to the Canadian Armed Forces' (CAF) No 410 Sqn on 27 October 1982, this unit serving as the Operational Training Unit (OTU) for the seven frontline fighter units that would subsequently receive Hornets.

CF-18s first saw combat during Operation *Desert Storm*, 18 jets from No 409 Sqn's Baden-Sollingen base having deployed to Doha, in Qatar, on 6 October 1990. Nicknamed the 'Desert Cats', the aircraft were manned by pilots from Nos 416 and 439 Sqns during the aerial campaign to free

◀ These two early-build CF-118Bs were amongst the first Hornets delivered to No 410 Sqn in 1984. The CAF was supplied with no fewer than 40 two-seaters, and these made up the majority of the 38 Hornets on charge with this squadron, which had operated as the OCU for frontline units for the past 27 years. (via Philip Jarrett)

Kuwait. The Hornets primarily provided air cover for Canadian and coalition warships during the deployment, but they also got to attack Iraqi positions in Kuwait and near Basra, in southern Iraq.

With a thawing of relations between East and West following the ending of the Cold War in 1991, three Hornet squadrons were disbanded and annual flying hours for aircraft and pilots reduced. In 2001, 79 CF-18s were identified for a mid-life update by Boeing Integrated Defense Systems at a cost of $2.6 billion. Similar to the work carried out on Marine Corps A-model jets to bring them up to F/A-18A+ standard, the aircraft received AN/APG-73 radar and numerous avionics systems improvements. Structural upgrades were also introduced, followed by a Centre Barrel Replacement (CBR) for key aircraft. The 'centre barrel'

is the crucial central part of the aircraft's fuselage that supports the wings and landing gear. This part may be replaced for crash damage, or because of the continual hard landing damage sustained by aircraft – particularly those involved in the 'controlled crashes' of carrier landings.

Canadian Hornets saw further action in the spring of 1999 when 18 jets were sent to Aviano air base, Italy, to participate in Operation *Allied Force*. The detachment, known as the 'Balkans Rats', flew 678 combat sorties totalling 2500 hours whilst committed to the conflict.

As this book is compiled, six CF-18s from No 425 Sqn have been heavily involved in Operation *Unified Protector*, the NATO-led aerial campaign enforcing the no-fly zone over Libya. Initially flying CAP missions from Trapani air base in Sicily, the Hornets quickly swapped AMRAAMs for GBU-12 LGBs and have started attacking key military and regime targets as NATO strives to oust Col Muammar Gadaffi's regime.

Australia selected the Hornet as its next generation tactical fighter and Mirage III replacement in October 1980, the F-16 again being the losing design. A $2.788 million deal covered the purchase of 57 F/A-18As (initially ordered as AF-18As) and 18 F/A-18Bs (AF-18Bs), and all but two of these aircraft were assembled at the Government Aircraft Factory site at Avalon Airport, Victoria. The first jets were built in St Louis, and these were handed over to the Royal Australian Air Force (RAAF) on 29 October 1984. They were flown to Australia in May of the following year and put into service with No 2 OCU at RAAF Base Williamtown, in New South Wales.

That same month the first Australian-assembled jet was accepted by the RAAF, with the last Hornet being handed over in May 1990.

Three frontline units would receive 16 Hornets each between August 1986 and May 1988, Nos 3 and 77 Sqns being based with No 2 OCU at Williamtown and No 75 Sqn operating from RAAF Base Tindal, in the Northern Territory. Routinely exercising with neighbouring air forces in Southeast Asia, as well as with the USAF's Pacific Air Force, a contingent of four RAAF Hornets from No 77 Sqn was sent to Diego Garcia, in the Indian Ocean, in November 2001 to provide CAP for coalition air assets based there. Codenamed Operation *Slipper*, this deployment allowed US and British fighters to be freed up for combat in OEF. The jets returned home in May 2002.

Did you know?
Swiss SF-18s have additional titanium used in their construction so as to allow them to achieve g-ratings of +9G if required, compared to a maximum of +7.5G for all other Hornets.

◀ F/A-18B A21-101 was the first of 75 Hornets built for the RAAF, the aircraft making its maiden flight from St Louis on 13 August 1984. Along with A21-102, this aircraft was ferried to Australia following a marathon 15-hour delivery flight on 16-17 May 1985. (via Peter Mersky)

In February 2003 a detachment of 14 Hornets was sent to Al Udeid, in Qatar, to support the coalition build-up of forces in the area ahead of OIF. Most of the aircrew and maintainers came from No 75 Sqn, although the jets were drawn from all operational units. Given the codename Operation *Falconer*, the RAAF Hornets initially flew DCA missions for 'high value' assets once the conflict commenced. When

◀ A No 75 Sqn F/A-18A takes on fuel from a 117th ARW KC-135R on 6 April 2003 during Operation *Falconer* – the Australian Defence Force's commitment to OIF. Fourteen Hornets spent three months conducting combat operations from Al Udeid air base, in Qatar, dropping 122 LGBs on Iraqi positions during that time. (RAAF)

it was clear that air superiority had been achieved, the Hornets were switched to CAS missions. By the time No 75 Sqn dropped its last bomb on 17 April, the unit had flown more than 350 missions and expended 122 LGBs.

Like the CAF, the RAAF commenced a $1.5 billion Hornet Upgrade Program for its jets from 2000, this project resulting in the Australian jets being equipped with many of the systems (including the AN/APG-73 radar) found in the F/A-18C/D Night Attack aircraft. Ten jets also had CBR work undertaken, with the last of these Hornets returning to service in October 2010. As with the CAF, the RAAF is scheduled to replace its F/A-18s with F-35C Joint Strike Fighters from 2020.

Spain's *Ejercito del Aire* (EdA) was the third, and last, air arm to receive

F/A-18A/Bs. Ordered as replacements for the F-4C, F-5A and Mirage III, Spain received 60 EF-18As and 12 EF-18Bs between July 1986 and July 1990. Issued to four frontline units (121 and 122 *Escuadrons* of *Ala de Caza* 12 and 151 and 152 *Escuadrons* of *Ala de Caza* 12) and a single OCU within the EdA, these aircraft have been used

▲ No 75 Sqn's Flg Off Mark Mohr-Bell peels away from an Omega Air Boeing 707-300 tanker during the aircraft's return trip to Australia following the completion of Exercise Bersama Shield 2010 *at Butterworth air base, in Malaysia. Some 59 military aircraft, 19 warships and 2500 personnel participated in this annual exercise, which is conducted by the Five Power Defence Arrangement over the Malaysian peninsula and the South China Sea in May-June. Note the wingtip-mounted AIM-132 ASRAAM training round, this weapon having replaced the AIM-9M in RAAF service from 2004. (RAAF)*

▲ An F/A-18A from No 3 Sqn prepares to take off from Darwin airport on 19 July 2010 during Exercise Pitch Black 2010. *This unit is usually based at Williamtown, New South Wales. (RAAF)*

► *These four EF-18Bs were flown non-stop from Lambert Field in St Louis to Zaragoza, Spain, with the aid of aerial refuelling on 10 July 1986. Their arrival marked the start of the EdA's acceptance of the Hornet into service. Prior to their delivery, the four aircraft had been used to train the first class of Spanish instructors at Whiteman air force base, Missouri. Three of these jets were assigned to 151* Escuadron *and the fourth to 152* Escuadron. *(via Peter Mersky)*

primarily in the all-weather interceptor role. From September 1992 a fleet-wide upgrade was instigated that made the jets NITE Hawk and AMRAAM compatible.

Did you know?

The F/A-18 CBR programme is a major engineering and overhaul procedure that extends the life of the centre fuselage beyond the original withdrawal date of the aircraft. The ten RAAF aircraft that were subjected to this process between 2003 and 2010 had their wings removed in Williamtown by BAE Systems Australia, after which the Hornet fuselages were airlifted to the L-3 CBR-dedicated facility in Mirabel, Canada, and then sent back to Williamtown for final assembly and returned to flight status by BAE.

Spanish Hornets had their combat debut in December 1994 when eight aircraft were deployed to Aviano as part of Operation *Deny Flight*. Flying CAP missions for their first five months in-theatre, two jets dropped LGBs on a Serbian ammunition dump in May 1995. Six months later Spanish EF-18s also expended HARMs in

SEAD strikes against the Serbian air defence network during Operation *Deliberate Force*. That same year 24 surplus US Navy F/A-18A/Bs were acquired by the EdA as interim replacements for the delayed Eurofighter Typhoon. Delivered between 1995 and 1998, these aircraft did not receive the subsequent software upgrades that were installed in the surviving EF-18s.

In March 1999 eight Hornets were committed to Operation *Allied Force*, these jets again flying from Aviano. Initially performing CAP for other NATO strike aircraft, the EF-18s quickly switched to the precision bombing role, employing LGBs. As this volume goes to press, four EF-18s have been flying combat missions over Libya from Decimomannu, on Sardinia, since late March 2011 as part of Operation *Unified Protector*. Like Canada and Australia, Spain

◄ *EF-18A C.15-59 was one of a pair of Spanish Hornets to attend the 2009 Royal International Air Tattoo at RAF Fairford. This aircraft hails from Torrejon-based Ala de Caza 12, which was formerly equipped with the Phantom II. (Chris Lofting)*

◄ *This EF-18A (C.15-16) returns to Florennes air base, Belgium, after completing a NATO Tactical Leadership Programme sortie in June 2008. Assigned to Ala de Caza 15 at Zaragoza, the aircraft has tiger-striped LERX fences which denote that the unit's badge features a white tiger. (Chris Lofting)*

is due to retain its Hornets through to at least 2020.

Kuwait was the first nation to purchase the F/A-18C/D Night Attack variant of

▲ These F/A-18Cs belong to No 9 Sqn (nearest and furthest aircraft) and No 25 Sqn. The latter unit specialises in air-to-ground and anti-shipping operations, while No 9 Sqn performs the air defence mission. Kuwaiti F/A-18Cs were involved in the early stages of OSW. (Peter Steinemann)

the Hornet, ordering 32 C-models and eight two-seaters in September 1988 as replacements for its A-4KU Skyhawks and Mirage F 1CKs. These jets were not, however, fitted with AN/APG-73 radar or made AMRAAM compatible. The first Kuwaiti Hornet flew on 19 September 1991 and deliveries to Kuwait International Airport commenced four months later. The last aircraft arrived on 21 August 1993, by which time the Hornet's permanent home of Ali al Salem air base had been rebuilt after being severely damaged during the Iraqi occupation of 1990-91. Assigned to Nos 9, 25 and 61 Sqns, the aircraft have since moved to Ahmed al Jaber.

No 25 Sqn specialises in air-to-ground and anti-shipping operations, No 9 Sqn is the air

defence unit and No 61 Sqn performs pilot training. Although routinely exercising with the air forces of neighbouring countries, and US Navy air wings operating with Fifth Fleet, the Kuwaiti Hornets have never seen combat. Kuwait is currently evaluating long-term replacement options for its Hornet fleet, with France's Rafale billed as a leading contender.

Finland became the next country to order the F/A-18C/D when, in May 1992, the nation's minister of defence announced that it had beaten off the F-16C/D as a replacement for the MiG-21bis and Saab 35F Draken fighters then in frontline service. Some 57 single-seaters and seven F/A-18Ds would be procured, with the bulk of these machines being assembled from

The F/A-18 Hornet has been the premier fighter aircraft of the Royal Australian Air Force for the last two decades. We operate this aircraft in a unique environment – Australia's vast landmass, and the inhospitable and sometimes unforgiving climate, present challenges and opportunities that other operators can only imagine. And the nations who fly the F/A-18 are many and varied, each with their own strategic imperatives and operational doctrine. Yet the one constant is that we have all embraced the combat power that this aircraft can deliver in the defence of our respective countries.

Air Marshal Angus Houston
Chief of the Air Force

▲ *An F-18C from HävLLv 31 takes off in full afterburner at the start of its display routine at the 2010 Midnight Sun Airshow in Kauhava, Finland. (Joerg Stange)*

kits in Finland by Valmet Aircraft Industry. Delivered between 1995 and 2000, the aircraft are designated F-18C/Ds in Finnish service due to the fact that fighter squadrons HävLLv 11, 21 and 31 fly them exclusively in the air superiority role. The jets still retained all the avionics for the air-to-ground mission, and during the third phase of the F-18's Mid-Life Upgrade Program in 2008, Litening targeting pods and JSOW glide bombs were

ordered. AIM-120C AMRAAM and AIM-9X Sidewinders were also acquired.

Switzerland became the penultimate Hornet customer when it ordered 26 F/A-18Cs and eight F/A-18Ds in June 1993. The Hornet had been chosen as a replacement for the Mirage III and Hunter five years earlier, but political changes in Eastern Europe saw the Swiss government delay the acquisition. Like the Finnish

A Hornet from Fliegerstaffel *17 deploys flares after making a strafing run on the Axalp-Ebenfluh weapons range in Switzerland in October 2007. (Joerg Stange)*

machines, these aircraft were assembled locally from kits by Schweizer Flugzeuge und System AG between 1996 and 1999. Designated SF-18C/Ds in Swiss service, the fighters are flown by *Fliegerstaffeln* 11, 17 and 18.

The last country to acquire the Hornet was Malaysia, which ordered eight two-seat F/A-18D Night Attack aircraft similar in configuration to US Marine Corps jets in July 1993. These were bought to replace F-5E/F Tiger IIs following the acquisition of F-16s by neighbouring Singapore and Thailand. Tasked with performing the strike and anti-shipping roles, all eight aircraft were delivered in 1997 to Butterworth-based No 18 Sqn. Malaysia also looked into buying 12 single-seat Hornets, but opted for 16 MiG-29Ns and two MiG-29NUBs instead.

◄ *The first of Malaysia's eight F/A-18Ds to be built, M45-01 made its maiden flight on 19 March 1997. Butterworth-based No 18 Sqn had completed its equipment with the aircraft by late August that same year. M45-01 is seen here taxiing past the squadron's 'carport' style shelters at Butterworth, on the northwest coast of the Malay Peninsula. (Peter Steinemann)*

▼ *M45-07 takes off from Butterworth at the start of a training mission. The Night Attack Hornets routinely exercise with RAAF F/A-18As from No 75 Sqn, which head north to Butterworth for Exercise* Bersama Shield. *(Peter Steinemann)*

F/A-18A HORNET

Crew:	pilot
Length:	56 ft 0 in (17.10 m)
Wingspan:	37 ft 6 in (11.46 m)
Wing Area:	400 sq ft (37.20 m^2)
Height:	15 ft 3 in (4.66 m)
Weights:	21,830 lb (9902 kg) empty and 51,900 lb (23,542 kg) maximum take-off weight
Service ceiling:	50,000 ft (15,250 m)
Maximum range:	575 nautical miles (1065 km)
Maximum speed:	1190 mph (1904 kmh)
Cruising speed:	660 mph (1056 kmh)
Engines:	two 16,000 lb st (72.70 kN) General Electric F404-GE-100 afterburning turbofans
Armament:	one M61A1 Vulcan 20 mm cannon with 570 rounds of ammunition, up to eight air-to-air missiles (AIM-9L/M/X Sidewinder, AIM-7F/M Sparrow and AIM-120C AMRAAM) on two wingtip, four underwing and two nacelle fuselage stations and up to 17,000 lb (7711 kg) of conventional ordnance

F/A-18C HORNET NIGHT ATTACK

Crew:	pilot
Length:	56 ft 0 in (17.10 m)
Wingspan:	37 ft 6 in (11.46 m)
Wing Area:	400 sq ft (37.20 m^2)
Height:	15 ft 3 in (4.66 m)
Weights:	23,832 lb (10,810 kg) empty and 56,000 lb (25,401 kg) maximum take-off weight
Service ceiling:	50,000 ft (15,250 m)
Maximum range:	575 nautical miles (1065 km)
Maximum speed:	1190 mph (1904 kmh)
Cruising speed:	660 mph (1056 kmh)
Engines:	two 18,000 lb st (81.80 kN) General Electric F404-GE-402 afterburning turbofans
Armament:	one M61A1 Vulcan 20 mm cannon with 570 rounds of ammunition, up to eight air-to-air missiles (AIM-9L/M/X Sidewinder, AIM-7F/M Sparrow and AIM-120C AMRAAM) on two wingtip, four underwing and two nacelle fuselage stations and up to 17,000 lb (7711 kg) of conventional ordnance

APPENDIX 2 – F/A-18 HORNET MILESTONES

1966

May – Northrop design the P-530 Cobra as a replacement for its F-5 lightweight fighter.

1972

January – The revised Northrop P-600 emerges as the definitive design from the company for the Light Weight Fighter (LWF) technology demonstration programme. The USAF formally commits to the new aircraft, issuing a request for proposals (RFP) on 6 January.

April – the USAF awards contracts to Northrop (YF-17) and General Dynamics (YF-16) to build two LWF prototypes.

1974

27 April – USAF LWF programme becomes the Air Combat Fighter (ACF) programme, aimed at developing a low cost, high performance tactical fighter.

9 June – YF-17 prototype makes its first flight from Edwards Air Force Base, California.

1975

13 January – The YF-16 defeats the YF-17 to win the USAF's ACF competition.

2 May – The Northrop/McDonnell Douglas team is chosen by the US Navy as prime contractor to develop the new F-18 strike fighter, which will enter service as the Navy Air Combat Fighter.

1978

18 November – the first of 11 Full Scale Development (FSD) F-18s makes its maiden flight from the McDonnell Douglas factory in St Louis, Missouri.

1979

30 October – FSD aircraft No 3 makes the Hornet's first carrier landing, aboard USS *America* (CV-66).

1980

10 April – Canada selects the F-18A as its new strike fighter, ordering 98 CF-18As and 40 CF-18Bs

1981

September – The first production F/A-18 is delivered to the US Navy's fleet replacement squadron, VFA-125, at NAS Lemoore, California.
20 October – Australia selects the F/A-18A/B as a replacement for the Mirage IIIO in RAAF service, acquiring 57 A/F-18As and 18 A/F-18Bs.

1982

December – the US Navy officially redesignated the Hornet the F/A-18 to emphasise its dual fighter and attack capabilities.
December – Spain orders 60 EF-18As and 12 EF-18s as F-4C, F-5A and Mirage IIIE replacements.

1983

January – The Hornet officially enters US operational service with Marine Corps squadron VMFA-314 at MCAS El Toro, California.

1985

February – VFA-25 and VFA-113, embarked aboard USS *Constellation* (CV-64), undertake the Hornet's first operational deployment.

1986

15 April – F/A-18As from VFA-132 and VMFA-323, flying from USS *Coral Sea* (CV-43), give the Hornet its combat debut when they fire HARMs at Libyan air defence targets.

1987

April – The 500th Hornet is delivered by McDonnell Douglas.
3 September – The first F/A-18C makes its maiden flight.

1988

22 January – The 380th, and last, F/A-18A for the US Navy and Marine Corps is delivered to VMFA-312.
6 May – The first F/A-18D makes its maiden flight.
September – Kuwait orders 32 F/A-18Cs and eight F/A-18Ds as replacements for its A-4KU Skyhawks.
October – Switzerland announces that it intends to order 34 Hornets, although a contract for their purchase is not signed until June 1993 due to political procrastination.

1989

14 November – The first F/A-18C Night Attack aircraft is delivered to the US Navy.

1990

10 April – The worldwide Hornet fleet surpasses one million flight hours.

1991

17 January – Flying bomb-laden F/A-18Cs, Lt Cdr Mark Fox and Lt Nick Mongillo of VFA-81 down two MiG-21s on the first day of Operation *Desert Storm*.

1992

May – Finland announces that it is to buy 57 F-18Cs and seven F-18Ds as MiG-21bis and Draken replacements.

1993

10 February – An F/A-18C is the 10,000th jet aircraft built by McDonnell Douglas.
July – Malaysia places an order for eight F/A-18D Night Attack aircraft.

1997

1 August – The merger between McDonnell Douglas and Boeing takes effect, with the new company being known as Boeing from now on.

1998

19 November – The 581st, and last, F/A-18C is delivered to the US Navy.

2000

31 August – The 192nd, and last, F/A-18D is delivered to the Marine Corps. Total production of the F/A-18A/B/C/D totals 1479 aircraft for eight customers.

2001

8 October – Hornets from USS *Enterprise* (CVN-65) and USS *Carl Vinson* (CVN-70) commence Operation *Enduring Freedom* with strikes on Taleban and al-Qaeda targets in Afghanistan.

2002

12 December – The worldwide F/A-18 Hornet fleet surpasses five million flight hours.

2003

March–April – More than 250 Hornets see combat in Operation *Iraqi Freedom* from carriers and land bases.

2004

August - The Marine Corps bases a full squadron of F/A-18s in Iraq, operating from Al Asad. This forward deployment is maintained until January 2010.

2006

September – Hornets from CVN-65's CVW-1 return to action over Afghanistan following an upsurge in anti-ISAF activity by the Taleban. F/A-18s have been a continual presence in the skies over the country ever since.

2008

September – Hornets from CVW-2, aboard USS *Abraham Lincoln* (CVN-72), conduct the final OIF missions flown by the F/A-18 over Iraq.

2010

June – VMFA-232s become the first Marine Corps unit to deploy to Kandahar as part of the 3rd Marine Aircraft Wing (Forward) commitment to OEF.

August – The US Navy is going to spend $7 billion to upgrade around 300 F/A-18A/B/C/Ds so as to lengthen their service lives by about 16 per cent to 10,000 flight hours. This will allow the Hornet to remain in fleet use through to 2030, the aircrafts' service lives having to be extended due to the slower-than-projected rollout of their replacement, the J-35C Joint Strike Fighter.

2011

February – The US Navy's F/A-18 programme manager, Capt Mark Darrah, is quoted as saying that the Hornet fleet is averaging about 330 flight hours per year, which means they are consistently about 30 per cent above planned usage due to ongoing combat operations in Afghanistan. Many have now exceeded even their extended usage figure of 8000 flight hours.

March – Canadian and Spanish Hornets are committed to Operation *Unified Protector*, flying strike missions over Libya.

◄ *F-35C flight test aircraft CF-1 formates with an F/A-18C from VX-23 overhead Patuxent River. Both the F-35C Navy variant and F-35B Marine Corps variant are being tested and evaluated at Pax River in preparation for delivery to the fleet from 2018. The Joint Strike Fighter is scheduled to replace all 'legacy' Hornets then still in service. (US Navy)*

▲ *Air department sailors assigned to the crash and salvage division of the aircraft carrier USS George H W Bush (CVN-77) spray water on an F/A-18A Hornet training aircraft during a flightdeck firefighting drill in July 2010. Surplus 'legacy' Hornets have fulfilled this role on both Pacific and Atlantic Fleet carriers for the past decade as more and more jets run out of airframe hours. (US Navy)*

Other titles available in this series

ISBN 978 07524 4399 4

ISBN 978 07524 4487 8

ISBN 978 07524 5080 3

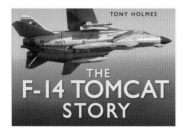

ISBN 978 07524 4985 2

ISBN 978 07524 5082 7

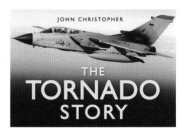

ISBN 978 07524 5085 8

Visit our website and discover thousands of other History Press books.
www.thehistorypress.co.uk